Cascades

General Editor: Geoff Fox

Talking in Whispers

Other titles in the *Cascades* series which you might enjoy are:

Jan Alone   Robert Leeson
The sequel to *It's My Life* takes a sensitive look at a young woman trying to come to terms with her emotions during the year after her mother's disappearance. Jan's life is now very demanding – running a home, looking after her young brother and working full time at the local factory, not to mention her relationship with her boss.

Hunter in the Dark   Monica Hughes
Mike Rankin is a boy who has everything – he's athletic, wealthy, and he can't wait to be sixteen. Then, it gradually becomes apparent that Mike is very ill, with a disease not even his parents will talk about . . .

The Owl Service   Alan Garner
There's a power stirring in a Welsh valley that dates from a sad and distant myth that forces Roger and Alison, stepbrother and sister, and Gwyn, the housekeeper's son, into a vicious predicament that looks likely to break up in violent disaster.

This story takes place in Chile, somewhere between the present and the future. The characters are the creation of the author but events such as those portrayed here have happened, are happening and will continue to happen, not only in Chile but in many countries where the force of arms rules the people instead of democracy and the rule of justice.

Today it's you who give the orders
What you say is said
And there is no argument
Today my people go around
Talking in whispers
Eyes on the ground . . .

In spite of you
Tomorrow will be
Another day.

Chico Buarque

One

In the great stadium of Santiago twenty thousand people lift hands and voices in salutation. Their chant rises as one voice:

'Mig-uel! Mig-uel!'

The afternoon sunlight frames the head of Miguel Alberti, the Silver Lion, as he stands to speak. He wears a white suit. In his hand he holds a green panama.

'People of Chile . . . Compañeros!' His arm is a spear, upraised. 'Comrades in hope.' Cheers roll under the caverns of the stadium like sea breakers. 'The Generals have promised to sheath their swords. We are once more winning the argument for democracy in this proud land . . . Tomorrow, the people of Chile will go to the elections. As sure as my hair is silver and my memory long, they will vote to send the soldiers back to their barracks—where they belong!'

The Silver Lion whirls his hat in the air. 'Freedom will be reborn. Not just for the few—but for all. The prison doors will open and the spirit of justice, and of equality, will fly forth with the strength of the condor!'

'Tomorrow—tomorrow!' chant the crowd.

Miguel, the people's choice for president, spins his hat high into the blue spring sky. It flutters. It hovers—a green bird of peace in silhouette against the massive grey wall of the Andes.

A sturdy arm reaches higher than a dozen others, a youth with a red and black band around his forehead, laughing with delight as he clutches the green dove. The crowd offer congratulations with drums and bugles as the youth waves the hat triumphantly and plonks it at a jaunty angle on the head of the girl beside him. 'Try this for size, Isa!' She turns and the sun catches the smiles of twin brother and sister.

'Tomorrow!' The girl lifts her brother's hand towards the sun. The crowd thunders its joy.

From tomorrow, all will be different.

Andres knew for certain that his friend Horacio was dead. The shots had pierced the side window of the car. There had been the swerve, no brakes applied, and then the ditch. Andres had been thrown clear, into the dusk of evening, but Juan, his father—they had got him, dragged him from the capsized vehicle.

Four of them, with guns.

They were searching for Andres now, among the brambles and scrub where the ground rose up from the winding valley road. He was a witness.

He had scrabbled along the ditch on hands and knees. It was littered with sharp rocks. He dug at the crisp topsoil, then powdered it over his face. He reached the first bend in the road. He lunged in among blackberry bushes.

All at once, the ditch and the slope above it were sprayed with machine-gun fire. Earth burst up into clouds. Trees spat bark.

'Come forward, boy—with your hands up!'

'There was no one else. Just the two of us.' That was Juan, trying to protect his son.

'We counted three. We followed you from the stadium, Larreta—we *know*.'

'Only my guitarist, Horacio Rivera, and myself. We dropped off my son.'

Through the gimlet space of the brambles, Andres saw his father beaten to the ground with the butt of the machine-gun. 'You, Larreta, will pay for your lies, and you'll suffer for your songs. The Minstrel of the People has given his last concert for the Silver Lion.'

Andres smelt earth, spring-dry, and the scent of pines. They were searching for him, rummaging through the brambles, kicking spaces, scraping boots against rocks, pushing rocks aside; rocks that rolled down gradients, bouncing towards the deep roar of the river.

Who are they? A Death Squad? More probably, Security. Our friends the CNI.*

'Hernandes?'

'Sir?' Very close.

'See to the car.'

Andres heard Hernandes grunt. He had scratched himself on the brambles. In revenge, he aimed a burst of gunfire into the shadows.

'What about the boy?'

'See to the car, we can't bullshit around all night.'

'He'll talk, Sir. They're that kind of family.' If Hernandes now chose to track leftwards, he would step on top of Andres who stuck his face in earth. He could hear his heart, his pulses.

'Not hair nor hide of him round here, Sir,' called another man. 'He probably caught one.' He too aimed into shadows and fired. 'That's two.'

Hernandes was reluctant to give up the chase. 'Unless he's a cat with nine lives.' He had looked left. He stared into undergrowth. He stared directly at Andres: he stared but he did not see. He spoke to the fugitive he sensed still breathed. 'There'll be a next time.'

'Hernandes—the car!'

Hernandes swore under his breath. He dropped down the slope to the Security car and took two tins of petrol from the boot. He opened the driver's door of Juan Larreta's old Chevrolet. He poured petrol over the body of Horacio. He drenched the musical instruments of Juan's trio, Los Obsti-

*Chile's secret police, formerly called the DINA.

11

nados—the Obstinate Ones. He turned the steering wheel. 'Give her a push.'

Two Security men pressed their weight behind the Chevy, manoeuvring it slowly to the edge of the road. Below, were rocks, a precipitous fall and then the river. 'Stand back.' Hernandes lit a match. He threw it into Horacio's face. 'Bloody redneck!'

Corpse and car were ablaze. The Security men gave the Chevy a final push. It tipped, burning, then exploded as it overturned. It angled out into space. It struck rocks and water simultaneously with a terrific bang.

Andres' last view of his father was of him being punched and kicked into the Security car. He watched it accelerate away in a wild sweep, dust shooting from its rear wheels, tyres howling as they met the tarmac of the road leading back to Santiago.

Andres stood as the pines, as the stone cliff above him. Tears of grief transformed the landscape to a sea-wash of greys and browns and fading blue. Horacio, whom he'd known since childhood, who'd been singing his new composition only instants before the bullet silenced him: gone for ever. And Juan, father, friend—best of companions— snatched away to the prisons of a living death.

I should have let myself be taken. There's no honour in this, skulking in brambles, with only a scratch to show for my bravery. If I'd given myself up at least I'd have driven with him. On the last journey.

He gazed down at his scratches, not one but many. Honour? He shook his head. Bravery? This happens, and all you can do is spout like a tight-ass recruit at the Military Academy. His mouth was caked with earth. He coughed violently.

He advanced several steps, out of the profound blackness of the shadows. At first glance, Andres' lanky frame looked frail; he was all sharp angles—bony shoulders, wide hips, protruding knees: everything suggested ungainliness. Yet in movement he cancelled out such an impression. He was lithe and balanced, light on his feet, agile, but most of all his physique suggested staying-power and resilience.

He glanced at the wrist-watch given him by his British-born mother, Helen. It had belonged to her Scottish father who had once—Andres never stopped boasting—played football for Glasgow Celtic. Andres had played midfield for his school team and had had a trial for Santiago Youth. His future, though, until this evening, lay with Los Obstinados.

In just over half an hour the Silver Lion was due to give his last election speech, in his home town of San José; and but for the action of the Security, Juan, Horacio and Andres would have been there too, with Braulio the drummer, to play at a celebration concert in the town square.

I must get to San José, fast. Tell Miguel what's happened to Horacio and Juan. He'll speak out. He'll shame the generals.

Andres climbed down to the river, keeping a distance from the still-burning Chevy half in the River Maipo, half out. He drank. He washed the disguise of dry-dust from his face—and then suddenly he stood up, listening intently.

Transport!

He clawed a route back up the river bank. Walking, this journey could take him all night. If I can thumb a lift—yet what driver in his right mind'll stop for a stranger in the dark? In Chile, these days.

Still, he tried to reassure himself, I'm no threat. Too skinny to scare anybody.

What Andres did not admit to himself was that his eyes, always intense, often fierce and challenging, would not assure strangers that to be in this young man's company was to be without risk. As Braulio used to say of Andres, 'You've got a stare that could make rivets melt.'

'That's because I feel things passionately.'

Braulio would nod approvingly, wisely. 'Just be careful

that with sparks like yours you don't set people alight.'

Braulio would be at San José, waiting, anxiously wondering. Sparks or no sparks, Andres needed this lift. He stepped out into the road, thumb held high.

An ancient van rattled up the hill towards him, wheels wobbling, one side-lamp unlit. With my extra weight inside, it'll probably need pushing. Andres eased back on to the grass verge as the van approached.

Will it, won't it?

He tried to peer in at the occupants. They weren't stopping. He shouted: 'Please!' The van passed, almost slow enough for him to jump aboard. He ran after it, waving. For a moment he thought the van was speeding up to escape him. Then, as though the driver had abruptly changed his mind, it pulled across the road and came to a halt beneath the dark shoulder of the hill.

Andres stopped running. He stood quite still. Don't scare them off. They're watching you through the rear mirror. He raised his hands to show that he carried no weapon.

Both of the van doors opened at once. A girl, and a youth with a bright-coloured hair-band, came round the van to look at him. The youth held a starting handle—just in case.

They had spotted the still-burning Chevrolet at the river's edge. 'That yours?' called the youth.

Andres was silent. In Chile under the military junta you trust the truth only with close friends. And sometimes not even then. 'Nothing to do with me . . . I missed my bus to San José.'

As they were obviously not going to come any closer, Andres took a careful pace forward, then a few more. He stopped before he became a threat. 'If you're heading that way, it'd be a great help.'

He saw that the youth and the girl were twins—identical twins. They were tallish, very handsome, proud despite their rickety old van. He was close enough to read the roughly-painted lettering on the side: MARIONETAS DE

LOS GEMELOS (Marionettes of the Twins).

'I think I've seen you.' He pointed at the sign. 'At the market of San Miguel.'

They were pleased. They exchanged smiles. The youth nodded. 'You're the first to see our new sign. It's in celebration of—'

'Ssh, Beto,' cautioned his sister.

'Oh what does it matter, Isa? He's not going to run and tell the CNI . . . are you, Señor?'

Andres shook his head. 'I remember you had a skeleton, with a skull that kept bouncing up and hitting people. And an ostrich—'

'Orlando—'

'That pecked people's noses.'

They all laughed, nervously, and the first seeds of trust were sown. Andres was invited to hop in among the twins' menagerie of puppets. There were more than a dozen of them, jiggling on long strings suspended from wooden racks built into the roof of the van.

'You're in luck,' said Beto, coaxing the van into life again and moving off. 'San José's precisely where we're heading. The town'll be packed for election day.'

'We hope to do at least three shows,' added Isa. 'You don't sing or dance, do you?'

'Dance? No. But I can sing a bit—play the charango.' Andres broke off. He was giving away too much to strangers. 'Well, anyway . . . I used to.'

Beto overcame Andres' embarrassment by ignoring it. 'Our company's planning to expand. We could do with a singer and a charango player.'

Andres did not answer. He was all at once choked with the memory of Horacio, the most talented guitarist and charango player in Chile, in all South America, Juan often said; and of Juan himself, sweetest of singers, who would soon be singing a song of another sort at the hands of the CNI.

15

Beto had not driven far before he pulled off the road into a lay-by scooped out of the hill. 'Supper. Care to join us?'

Andres concealed his impatience to get to San José without delay. And anyway, he was famished. Isa reached between her feet. 'It's not much.' She snapped a long crisp loaf into three, sliced the pieces and inserted circles of garlic sausage. She dropped a tomato and a wedge of cheese into Andres' hand.

'Beer?' Beto flipped the rubber cork from a litre bottle. He stared at Andres as he handed him the beer. 'If I poke a lot of questions at you, my sister'll do a kneecap job on me.' He paused. He waited.

And Andres waited, uncomfortable.

'We've got a great conversationalist here, Sis.'

'Eat up and shut up.'

Beto whistled. 'Yes, boss . . . You wouldn't think, would you, stranger, that I entered this world nine and a half minutes before Big Momma here? Which *should* have qualified me to wear the pants in this family.'

Andres did not care for the impression he was giving—defensive, untrusting, without warmth. He smiled. 'I'm an only child. I'd have liked a brother or a sister.'

'Sisters are born bullies.' Beto did not mean it seriously. His wink indicated that this was a line he took in order to provoke a lively argument. 'They're always so generous with advice.'

Andres turned to Isa. 'And brothers, what are they like?'

Isa's face reminded him of the painting of an Inca princess he had seen in Peru, in a palace that soared into the kingdom of the clouds; a princess with large, solemn and distant eyes. Her hair was in two plaits curled up round her ears like rams' horns.

He sensed the strength in her silence. Yet her voice was mellow and humour touched the corners of her mouth as she spoke. 'Brothers take running jumps at things—and then think about the distance when it's too late.'

Beto gave a vigorous nod of assent. 'Exactly. If she'd had her way, that sign on the van would have had to wait till the Silver Lion won the elections. So I told her—it's in the bag, and up went the sign.'

'Do *you* think it's in the bag?' Isa asked Andres.

'I was beginning to believe it was.'

Beto switched on the cab light. He looked hard at Andres. 'I've been puzzling ever since we picked you up.' He glanced at his sister. 'We've seen him some place, haven't we?'

Isa switched off the light. 'There you go again.'

Beto's curiosity was in full flow. He gave a tweak to Andres' cord bomber jacket. 'You're a Towny, that's for sure . . . a student?'

'Beto!'

'Okay.' Beto relented. He started up the engine, though his eye was still on Andres through the rear mirror. 'Well I can tell you this, Towny—if I *think* we've seen you, Isa *knows* we have.'

They drove under stars on a winding route that crossed and re-crossed the river. Farm hamlets lay black in sleep; copses of pine shaped the skyline. And always, against the drone of the van's engine as it laboured through the gears, came the roar of the Maipo, amplified by the walls of the canyon.

Suddenly the road ahead of them was blocked. At the entrance to a village that narrowed the route to no more than the width of two cars, several vehicles stood in a motionless tailback. Beyond was a crowd of people, almost silent, as though they had gathered for a funeral procession.

Beto halted in line. 'Now what?'

The drivers had got out of their vehicles. They were talking to people in the crowd, all staring or pointing away out of the village as if the source of their concern lay in the direction of San José. Beto got down. 'I'll see.'

He followed the dip in the road, past the first cars in line

17

and went to the perimeter of the crowd. Isa and Andres watched him as he spoke to a villager. They observed his instant response to what he was told—of shock, of anger. He raised his arms, grief-stricken.

Beto came racing back. As he ran, he shouted the news. It blunted against the silence. He did not repeat his message till he was abreast of the cab. He flung in the words: 'The Silver Lion's been shot dead. At San José . . . Dead! He was making his speech . . .'

Andres clipped his hands to his eyes. He felt the breath gush out of him. Only hours ago, he had shaken hands with the gentle philosopher-poet, the man who had defied the threats of the Junta, who had scorned the Death Squads, who had roused the people with his golden oratory.

'They've blamed the Communists,' said Beto, unbelieving. He was in tears.

The village crowd had opened a path for two policemen on motorcycles. The crowd was ordered to disperse. The police began to check the documents of the drivers in the tailback.

Beto put the van into reverse. He backed up the road a few metres. He turned. He watched the police through his wing mirror. He was shaking. 'We've got to decide what to do . . . Now, everything's changed—everything!'

Beto pulled off the road on to a farm track behind a protective curve of pines. He climbed out and the others followed, at a distance, keeping their distance.

It was Isa's way, as it was Andres', to take bad tidings in silence; yet Beto's way was to talk out his pain. 'I'll leave Chile . . . Go to Europe—I can't stand this. Not Miguel's death. Another good man, another Allende—buried!'

Beto dropped to the ground. In his anguish, he ripped at the earth. He threw the soil about him like a mad dog hustling for a lost bone. He stopped only when Isa went to him, raised him to his feet, put her arms under his arms and rested her head against his.

'What'll we do, Isa?'

'We must go back to town. Now.'

'But in the future, I mean?' His eyes went past his sister to Andres. He spoke to his sister. 'Who is he, Isa?'

Her gaze and his were one. She turned the question. 'What will you do? Our route lies back to Chago.'

Andres was desolated. He had no words. No plans. He shrugged. 'Just drop me off.'

Isa made a decision for all of them. She took Beto by the arm. 'Towny will spend the night with us at the mill. We'll leave thinking till tomorrow.'

On the journey back to Santiago, they listened to the van radio. The military authorities had taken over all broadcasting stations. One message was repeated over and over again: the death of Miguel Alberti was a tragedy for the nation. The elections fixed for tomorrow would be postponed indefinitely. In the meantime, the people of Chile were urged to keep calm:

'The Junta declares a State of Emergency to come into effect immediately. Until further notice all public assemblies are banned. For a limited period only, the activities of political parties and trade unions will be suspended.

'From tomorrow a curfew will operate in all towns and cities in the Republic, extending from 21.00 hours to 06.00 hours each day. Those persons without special passes, seen abroad between forbidden hours, will be liable to arrest.'

The newsreader had paused for a moment as the first chords of the Chilean national anthem signalled the end of his broadcast.

'People of Chile—the price of honour and justice is eternal vigilance. The Resistance Movement must be crushed once and for all. Let us therefore stand together, in unity, against the enemy within.

'This broadcast comes to you by order of His Excellency General Zuckerman, commander of the armed forces, President of the Republic.

'God Bless Chile!'

It was not until Beto, Isa and Andres had reached the south western outskirts of the city that they heard the gunfire. Beto celebrated. 'People are fighting back! Maybe the Resistance has climbed out of its mothballs.'

Andres strained his ears and his eyes: the sounds of combat were sporadic—a burst of machine-gun fire, an answering crack of rifles, then a deeper, more powerful thud of shells. 'Those are tanks.'

Beto slowed the van. The road had been deserted but now it was busy with traffic—most of it racing in the opposite direction, out of the city. 'What do we do, go back to Puente Alto and doss down for the night?'

'Press on, I'd say,' suggested Andres. 'Before they stick up road blocks.'

'And get blown to bits on the Alameda?'

'He's right, Beto,' said his sister. 'If we turn round now we'll only have to face the same problem in the morning.'

'That gunfire's straight ahead.'

'Then turn east. Not every street in San Miguel will be a battlefield.'

'That's what I'd hoped you'd say.' Beto speeded up. 'If I'd suggested it, you'd have called me a hot-head.'

The street lights were out. Only traffic signals shed any illumination in the black, deserted city. The van had been threading a quiet route, in third gear, sometimes second, through a maze of narrow streets when Beto braked hard. 'Cristo!' Andres pitched against the front seat. The puppets slithered along their runners.

The gunfire had re-opened its clash with the night directly in front of them, a street away. 'We're in the thick of it!' Beto crashed the gears into reverse. The van stalled.

Nothing for the moment was visible: the combatants

were firing along the line of the junction of roads. Yet the gunfire was so close and so intense that it seemed no longer ahead, where the streets crossed, but all around them.

And then, as though somebody had thrown an electric switch, the fury of sound ceased. There was an uncanny hush, a waiting, a probing: was the enemy dead; was there any further need of bullets; was the action over?

'Wh-what do we do?' asked Beto in a whisper and a lather of sweat.

Isa unlatched her door. 'Take shelter, I think.'

'Leave everything?'

'They only need to come round that corner,' warned Andres.

Together, they left the van, high and dry in the middle of the road, engine still ticking with heat. They found refuge in a garden porch, third house along from the street corner. A pungent smell of eucalyptus hung in the darkness.

The rival armies—if they still existed—held their fire. The intruders held their breath. Far off, towards the city centre, there was more gunfire. From the north came the sound of planes, of helicopters.

Beto challenged the silence. 'What's keeping them?' He turned to his companions. 'This is getting us nowhere, hanging about. Somebody . . . somebody ought to take a look—up there.' His proposal was not greeted with wild enthusiasm by the others. 'After all, I've done the driving.'

Andres felt, in Beto's mind, he had been volunteered for the job. 'Stick my head round the corner, do you mean?'

'If it's clear, we get moving.'

Isa was brisk, decisive. 'I'll do it.' She left them, only for Andres to overtake her to the second house porch. 'You stay.'

'No.' It was Andres' turn to be resolute. 'Because I owe it to you. And to my Dad.' He was already sprinting to the last house. He was not more than ten strides from the corner. Here's praying. He wondered—am I really doing this for Dad, for glory or just to show off in front of this dream of a girl, proving I'm as brave—or as stupid—as Beto?

Another second and I might go on to prove how much deader I can be than Beto.

He was at the very joining edge of the street. He noticed that where his flattened palm took comfort from solid walls of stone, there was a spray-canned message in white letters:

SAVE THE JUNTA TIME AND BULLETS—SHOOT YOURSELF!

Andres hesitated to look round the corner of the building. But Isa, right behind him, nudged him into action. He eased his right eye into the open—his eye told all a fraction of an instant before his ears took up the story.

The cross-street stage crashed open with the roar of steel tracks over stone.

'Tanks!'

His voice was a shout, for nothing but a bomb would have penetrated the din of cannon fire which now raddled the streets. He hurled himself away from the corner, against Isa, taking her to ground with him. 'Head down!'

For seconds only: they were too exposed. They scrambled. They ran. The gunfire became so deafening, so touchable, that it seemed to have thrown a wall around them, first barring their escape, then capsizing over them.

Three tanks, two forward, one to the rear, clanked and droned from left to right, and after them came a score of infantrymen ducking behind the reinforced steel of their riot shields.

Andres, Isa and Beto had gathered, in numbed helplessness, in full view of the soldiers—in full view that is if one of them should as much as turn his head. Yet the viewing slits of the tanks and the eyes of the soldiers remained fixedly forward. The three statues of flesh shook, gasped—but were not seen. Isa was first to move as the last of the soldiers passed from stage left to stage right. 'Into the van.'

Mouth open, goof-eyed, Beto was still half-buried in a dream of bricks and bullets. 'But . . .'

'No buts—we go!'

Beto obliged. In the driving seat he switched on the ignition. 'We'll die . . .'

Isa commanded: 'Not reverse—forward.'

'Across that? Are you mad? Tell her, Towny, she's mad.'

Andres was as terrified, as shattered as Beto was. Yet he shrugged. 'Try it.'

'If you'd like me to drive, Beto,' Isa said softly, guile-fully, 'you could bunk down in the back.'

Beto wiped his mouth, but revved the van. 'The way you want it is the way we'll have it.' He plunged down on the accelerator.

'God bless the Silver Lion—and God bless us!'

Two

The gates of the National Stadium in Santiago have been opening and closing all through the night. The streets leading to the stadium are cordoned off by armoured cars. Those living close by are not allowed out of their homes because of the curfew; but from their shadowy windows, as dawn lifts over the Andes, they are able to watch the covered trucks entering the stadium in endless convoy.

On board the trucks are human cargoes, each batch of prisoners escorted by guards with machine-guns. The gates open and the vast empty stomach of the stadium swallows up the prisoners.

Somewhere beneath one of the main grandstands an officer has ripped the name of the stadium manager from his office door. He replaces it with a notice in large capitals: INTERROGATION CENTRE.

He calls to a guard. 'I'll take the foreign vermin first.'

The scream woke Andres. It was his own scream. In his nightmare, he was nine again. Two days off his ninth birthday, to be exact. He saw the pistol, aimed from a moving car. He saw his mother fall. He saw her fall and he saw the car speed away.

When Andres rushed to her she did not known him. One second—and gone. The White Knights—did they do it? The killer squads who had been threatening Juan with his own death if he continued to sing songs attacking the rich, attacking the generals for their tyranny?

Before his very eyes, Helen—Highland Helen as Juan called her—with her back to the road, a tree to the side of her in full summer leaf. Half-turned at a call, struck in the throat and heart.

They never found out. She was buried and there was no evidence, no clues. The police did not care. But the people at the hospital where she nursed—they came, they crowded the graveside; the hospital for the poor, until the Junta had shut it down.

Of course the Security too were at the graveside: they took the names of all the mourners.

At the sight of her, fallen, how he had raged. How he had yelled and wept. He had flung himself towards the ambulance. He would have been carried along by it had not the men relented, allowed him beside his dead mother, let him cover her with his arms.

He came to, not in the ambulance, not by the graveside where Juan, Horacio and Braulio had sung Helen to earth, but on a mattress on a sloping wooden floor. He saw bars, high up, filtering pale light.

'Steady does it, Towny. It's only us—Beto and Isa. You got a parting in your hair from a stray bullet. You were lucky.'

It hurt. Andres raised a hand to his head. There was a huge sticking plaster just below the line of his hair. 'That close!'

Beto grinned. 'You should have seen the hole it made in the van.' He patted Andres arm. 'Don't fret. We checked your brain—it's still intact.'

Andres felt as if he had been crowned with a red-hot poker. He moved and he was suddenly dizzy. He lay back. 'Was I raving?'

'Not a bit,' asserted Beto unconvincingly.

'Just a little,' admitted Isa. 'But what does it matter? You're among friends.'

'Thanks.'

25

Andres stared about him: bare, whitewashed walls; a slit window; just this mattress on the gnarled wooden floor; a workbench; puppets, still skeletons of wood, hanging from crossed-wood frames; freshly-painted stage backdrops spread round the walls. 'This your own place?'

'It's home . . .' Isa poured out a dish of soup from a pan simmering on a camping stove. Beto helped lever Andres into a sitting position, back against a wall that had shed much of its plaster to reveal the wood beneath.

'A mill?'

Beto explained. 'Three-tenths of a mill. The rest was bombed in '73 after they got rid of Allende. We've this old storeroom to sleep, eat and squabble in, and a place underneath for the van.'

'Plus a view of the city as fine as any you'd get from San Cristóbal,' added Isa.

'Nobody knows we're here, of course. We ship in our water, our own oil lamps. And so far—touch wood—we're left in peace.'

The twins watched Andres as he ate his soup. Beto rocked forwards and backwards on an upturned box, glancing from sister to guest. 'Can I tell him, Sis?' he asked eventually. 'I've to push off to the laundry in a minute, so . . .'

'Secrets?' asked Andres.

'Quite the opposite—young Señor Larreta. Quite the opposite.'

'You guessed.'

Isa knew all along. But you were still on the tip of my tongue . . . until this morning's paper. You're famous!' Beto reached behind him and brought out a copy of *The Mercury*. 'If this rag is to be believed—Andres, isn't it?— then we are at this minute nattering to a ghost. Here, read your own obituary—page two, below the fold.'

Andres put down his soup, trying to stay calm. He scanned the front page headlines:

JUNTA STEPS IN TO SAVE COUNTRY AFTER
REDS SLAY ALBERTI
ELECTIONS POSTPONED INDEFINITELY
CHILE UNDER CURFEW

He turned to page two. There was a blurred photograph of Los Obstinados, pictured giving a street performance—Juan singing, Horacio with guitar, Braulio on drums. The headline read: CAR DEATH OF BALLAD SINGER JUAN LARRETA.

In smaller type he learned of his own journey into the next world: Vehicle in flames on San José road. Larreta's son, Andres, and other members of Los Obstinados—Horacio Rivera & Braulio Altuna—die in fire.

The Mercury went on: According to police evidence, Larreta had been drinking heavily. A well-known alcoholic, he had refused medical assistance on numerous occasions.

Andres fought to hold his anger as the lies continued: Larreta's popularity as a singer had been in serious decline since the death of his British-born wife, Helen, seven years ago. Larreta claimed that his wife was shot by a so-called 'Death Squad', but the facts later proved that she had taken her own life.

Andres lunged from the mattress only to stumble over against Isa; his head burnt; his brain spun.

With firm but gentle hands Isa eased him back on the mattress. 'Do you expect the lap-dog of the generals to publish the truth?' He felt her palm cool against his forehead.

Soothed, Andres read on. He smiled. 'As a matter of fact, *The Mercury*'s got something right for once.' He read out the final paragraph:

'Larreta's sixteen year old son Andres had himself been in trouble lately with the authorities. He was expelled from his senior school for subversive activities: he was chairman of a

Human Rights Committee, linked with Amnesty International. The Committee was declared illegal three months ago following a banned march on the Ministry of the Interior, demanding news of political detainees.'

'Well, Isa,' said Beto, 'it looks as though we've given bed and board to a real barrel of trouble.' He folded his arms. 'You're gelignite, Towny—so even if you're not dead, you'd better pretend to be for the next few weeks.'

'You can stay here as long as you like,' offered Isa.

'But you must stay put. Head down, nose in, mouth shut.'

Andres shook his head. 'You've been great friends—I'm deeply grateful. But I've things to do. I can't disappear into the woodwork till it's all over. My father has many friends. My job's to tell them what's happened, to get them to help.'

'The Security know you're not dead, Andres,' said Isa. 'They'll watch for you. They'll tail you. Whoever you go to, you'll put in danger.'

'If I'm tailed, I'll stop. Please understand!'

Though he was late for work at the laundry, Beto sat down again. 'We do understand. Only too well—searching and searching, but never finding.' He was almost in tears and Isa took his hand, folding it into her own.

She explained: 'Our parents, our uncle, a cousin . . . they used to run the puppets. They must somehow have caused offence.'

'They disappeared,' Beto burst in, 'and we've never heard of them since. Not a thing!'

'How long ago?'

'Eighteen months. Every day for a year we went to the offices. Nobody knew anything. Nobody cared a damn.' Beto was up. 'I've got to go . . . I'm sorry for you, Andres. I'm sorry for us. Because there's nothing worse than waiting and waiting and not knowing.' He spat the words: '*They* know that! If people just disappear, you don't have to

28

try them. You don't need evidence against them. You don't even need to feed them in prison. And now I'm off.'

Beto left a silence as vast as the desert in the Big North. Andres watched Isa go to the workbench. She had finished dressing a new puppet. She held it up. It was a metre in length, a male figure in military uniform festooned with medals. The face was wide, swarthy, with a waxed moustache and bushy black eyebrows. 'Meet General Zuckero!'

The General danced into life, and out came a fruity and uncannily accurate imitation of the voice of the President of Chile. 'Friends and countrymen—you can tell the number of enemies there are in our midst by a very simple device. You count the detestable litter that is flung everywhere in our city. Until the litter-louts own up—we arrest everybody!'

Andres laughed. 'You plan to use him?'

'What do *you* think? One shake of his leg in public and we'd be inside the House of Laughter for the rest of eternity.'

'Yet you made him just the same.'

'After a while, you come to hate talking in whispers.'

Andres stared at Isa. 'Do you know what the luckiest thing is that's happened to me in the last few hours?'

Her eyes met his. She read his thoughts. 'That's what I feel too.'

The next morning, early, Andres set out under heavy rain-clouds to call on Juan's friends and to tell Horacio's family of his death. He walked for half an hour before he sighted any part of the city that he recognised.

The gun battles of two nights before between the military Junta and Resistance fighters seemed to have become ancient history as the shops opened for trade, as traffic got into its usual jams, as shutters rattled up, as sun awnings were levered into place.

And yet, thought Andres—nobody's looking into any-

29

body else's face. Today we are talking in whispers, eyes on the ground. The words from a song by Chico Buarque returned to Andres as he walked through a city which, just below the surface, was riven with fear:

Today it's you who give the orders
What you say is said
And there is no argument
Today my people go around
Talking in whispers
Eyes on the ground . . .

The song, though, was not one of despair. It was one of hope, an inspiration to resistance. How did it go?—yes:

You're going to pay double
For every tear shed
From this sorrowing of mine
In spite of you
Tomorrow will be
Another day . . .

The words cheered Andres; they sharpened his purpose. I'm not alone. I've always got to remember that—I'm not alone!

His journey skirted the district of Providencia, one of the wealthiest areas of the city. He noted angrily the number of national flags waving in celebration of the Junta's 'victory' from elegant, second-storey windows.

And here, Ladies and Gentlemen, among the toffs of snob-hill, we have the General Zuckerman fan-club. He's the very Model of a Modern Military Man; on Sunday he saves the nation; on Monday he murders his enemies; on Tuesday he'll torture the innocent; on Wednesday—well, never mind what he'll be up to on Wednesday.

For a moment Andres watched the flags curl in a strengthening wind from the Andes: a storm wind. Okay folks, you can unlock your jewel boxes and your bank vaults—the Silver Lion is dead!

Along the Avenida Bernardo O'Higgins, called the

Alameda because it was once lined with hundreds of poplar trees, there were tanks and armoured cars at every road junction. Yet what struck Andres about the centre of town was the air of normality. Apart from the guns, you'd think nothing had happened.

The streets were bustling with people. The fashionable shopping centres were doing business as usual. The car horns of impatient drivers were as noisy as ever. Andres was not sure whether he should be amazed, angry or simply resigned that, scarcely twenty-four hours after the murder of Miguel Alberti, the people's choice for a civilian president, the people should now be gazing in shop windows, drinking coffee at pavement cafes, trying on new hats, eating ice-cream.

He stared at the world as it passed and his eyes grew more fierce, the knot of anger inside him more tight. Saturday night, my father was kidnapped; today, where is he—what has happened to him? Am I the only one that cares?

As if expecting an answer, Andres looked up at the white statue of the Virgin Mary that adorned San Cristóbal, the great hill dominating the heart of Santiago. The sky had darkened. It was going to rain. Perhaps that was a sign of the Madonna's displeasure.

And there was another sign: ahead of him, Andres saw two soldiers of the Black Berets cross the street and make towards a youth with long, shoulder-length hair. They called to him. At first he did not hear them, did not notice them. Their boots, quickening over the pavement, caused the youth to glance round. Immediately, he started to run.

Andres felt his own legs quickening. He'd better stop! The youth crashed into pedestrians coming in the opposite direction. He sidestepped off the pavement. The traffic was heavy and forced him to head along the gutter. The Black Berets screamed at him to stop, surrender. The crowd seemed indifferent to the chase. Some merely made way.

Others protested, tried to shove the youth into the road with their arms.

One of the soldiers stopped. He raised his rifle. His warning voice was swallowed in the roar of the traffic. He fired. The youth was hit in the middle of the back. His arms went out. The impact of the bullet carried him off balance. He reeled towards the pavement. A second bullet struck him in the head and carried him straight into an oncoming taxi.

Andres was among the crowd, but his voice came pitching out of it, shrill, shaken: 'You murderers!'

The taxi had skidded, carrying the body of the youth over the pavement and into a row of passers-by. Ignoring the carnage, one Black Beret dragged the dead youth by the collar from the bonnet of the taxi.

The second Black Beret turned on his accuser, on Andres, who had dared to voice the thoughts of all those who had witnessed his cold-blooded execution of an innocent young man.

He encountered a sea of blank and horrified faces. Swifter than he had ever been on the football field, Andres had turned, moved, cut left and become a window-shopper under the blue awning of one of Chago's most expensive jewellers.

He was breathing hard as though he had been chasing the funicular to the top of San Cristóbal. Idiot! He accused himself of risking his life pointlessly. Yet he answered himself. Somebody had to say it.

He scrutinised the events going on behind him by watching their reflection in a huge silver trophy in the jeweller's window. The Black Berets were bundling the dead youth into the taxi.

Andres recognised the trophy. It was the Two Hemispheres Cup soon to be played for by teams from South America and Europe. He felt a wretched sadness. In his top drawer at home, he had tickets for the first match, between

Chile and England. He had looked forward to the tournament for months.

There was also a ticket for Juan: and Juan's seat would be empty. And a ticket for Horacio.

And Braulio—the maddest-keen football fan in all Latin America, would his seat at the stadium be empty too?

Andres swung round. There were tears in his eyes. He saw the slumped remains of somebody's son. All at once, it was too much. Still with the scene before him, he retreated several steps. Then he about-turned. He slipped through the crowd, unnoticed.

He headed north, to the poorer quarter, and to Horacio's place. As he walked, the rain began. It seemed to carry the salt of the far-off Pacific. With it came a freshness which Santiago only ever seemed to experience when the rain fell and dismissed the smog that hung over the city in a perpetual cloud.

In his sadness, in his wetness as the rainstorm burst over him, Andres recalled lines by Chile's greatest and most loved poet, Pablo Neruda:

> Do you want to be the lone ghost walking by the sea
> blowing his pointless, disheartening instrument?

Andres nodded, wiping the rain from his eyes. Is that how I'll end up—a lone ghost walking by the sea? And yet how did the poem go on?

> someone would come perhaps
> someone would come,
> from the crowns of the islands, up from the red sea
>   depths
> someone would come, someone indeed would come.

No answer. Not someone. Not anyone.

Andres had pressed the doorbell of the little terraced house where Horacio lived with his parents, his grandparents, brother and three young sisters. Usually one ring would summon eager heads from the windows, the door, round the corner, up the street—but now all was silent and deserted.

The rain had become torrential. The sky had dropped a grey darkness over the rooftops, making all but the foothills of the Andes disappear. Andres rang again several times. He noticed a movement from next door. A side window slipped gingerly open.

Andres tried a smile. 'Buenas dias, Señora! I'm Señor Rivera's friend. I've an important message for his family.'

The old woman's eyes were as narrow, as suspicious as the slit of window. 'The men were arrested last night.'

'Not the grandfather?' The old woman nodded. 'But he was eighty!'

'They give the women a beatin' too. Gone to relatives.'

'Do you know where, Señora?'

She shook her head. 'Not my business.' She wouldn't have told him even if she'd known. She closed her window. He turned to go. Her phrase haunted him: not my business. I wonder how often I'll be hearing that again.

Thus began Andres Larreta's miserable pilgrimage. He had drawn up a list of names. After Horacio's family came Braulio's, then those of Juan's friends in the city. The message was simple—Juan is still probably alive; please help me fight for his release.

At Braulio's whitewashed corner house in the Turkish Quarter—where there were plenty of Arabs but no Turks—there was no answer to Andres' knock and no old lady to report on the destiny of Braulio's wife, Anna.

The view through the letterbox told Andres that Braulio's home had also been on the list of the Security forces. It was wrecked: furniture overturned, plates and glasses hurled across the room, drawers emptied, their contents scattered in all directions. The hallway was littered with books, manuscripts, photographs.

On a single white sheet of paper close to the door was a spot of blood. Andres grieved, as much for his own home as

Braulio's. He thought of his own precious things—his books, his records, his charango, his new camera which Juan had bought him only weeks ago for his birthday; and the photo albums Andres had been compiling of his trip—with Los Obstinados—to Peru.

Everything precious, they destroy.

For several minutes Andres sat under the porch out of the rain. It was Braulio who had taught him how to play the charango, a small folk instrument like a guitar. Very thoughtful, Braulio, very silent until something angered him, or amused him. Then the friendly giant would explode like petrol in a bottle, flush red as these geraniums being battered by the rain, wave his arms like a windmill and go round lifting everybody off the ground as if they were sacks of wool.

Braulio could bend nails with one hand. He could hold four billiard cues between his fingers and thumb and lift them till they were parallel with the floor. Yet it was gentle Braulio who, stung on the back of his hand by a wasp, allowed the creature to withdraw its sting and fly away. Andres laughed at the memory, for Braulio had proved allergic to wasp stings and spent a week in bed afterwards, missing two concerts and a match for the Musicians' Soccer eleven against an Actors' eleven.

Where are you now, Braulio—hiding out in San José? Over the border, or locked up by the CNI, awaiting stings far worse than a thousand wasps could give you?

Andres told himself he must move on, catch the names on his mental list before they too disappeared in the rain. Yet he did not budge. The vision of the youth with the long hair, shot from behind, hurled itself back at him over and over again.

He'd done nothing—except be afraid. Was it just his long hair that had made the soldiers pick on the youth? Was long hair somehow another threat to the State?

Andres buried his face in his arms which crooked like

fortress walls around his knees. It would be so easy to despair, to accept the real and horrible fact that he would never see his father again. He looked up. The street was like a river.

He suddenly noticed he was being watched. He stared across the street at a stocky, elderly man, swathed in a cycle cape. Like Andres, he was sheltering from the storm under a house porch. He was of Indian stock, an Araucanian Indian, the most ancient of all Chile's inhabitants, and once the fiercest people in the whole continent of South America.

The strangers gazed at each other across the river. Andres felt a bond between them. You lost your kingdom to the Spaniard. I've lost my father. A thought stirred in him and provided a flicker of hope.

This street—it could be the Araucanos' river, the Bío-Bío, the frontier they defended against the Spanish conquerors for three hundred and fifty years—one of the longest wars in history. And peace didn't come till 1888 after the Indians had been practically wiped out.

Now the Araucanos were scattered throughout Chile, the men often working in bakeries, the women as domestic servants. They had lost everything.

'Yes,' Andres said aloud, raising a hand in friendly signal to the old man across the new Bío-Bío. 'Everything but their pride.' He stood up, glad to see his gesture returned. 'All right—if the Araucanos could fight their corner for three hundred and fifty years, it's high time Andres Larreta risked getting his feet wet.'

Feet truly squelching, clothes drenched and dripping down his skin, Andres scoured the city in search of Juan's friends. And his failure was total. It was as if, at the abduction of Juan Larreta, everyone who knew him had also vanished into thin air.

Occasionally Andres was admitted into homes by fearful wives, mothers, daughters, and the answers were always the same: He was arrested . . . He has taken cover . . . We have heard nothing. Although there was much sympathy for Andres' plight, people were relieved—sometimes eager—to see him leave.

He was trouble. He knew it. He understood.

I am an outcast.

The offices of Juan's music publisher had been shut down. The company which recorded his songs carried on its front door a handwritten note announcing suspension of business till further notice.

Andres went round the back of the building and found a caretaker emptying rubbish. The exchange was brief:

'You're Larreta's lad—get the hell out of here while you can!'

'He's alive—not smashed up in a car crash like *The Mercury* said. I've got to get people to rally round, petition for his release.'

'Hopeless, son. Everybody who knew him will have been on the hit-list too. My boss was snatched this morning.'

'Where do you think he'll have been taken?'

The caretaker replaced the dustbin lid as though it were strapped with explosive. He whispered so that even the warehouse cat could not eavesdrop. 'I guess by now the prison ships'll be bursting at the seams, like last time. So it's a toss-up. If your father's lucky, it'll be the National Stadium.'

Andres wiped the soggy hair from his eyes. 'And if he's not lucky?'

The caretaker drew a finger-blade across his throat. 'Then it'll be the House of Laughter, God keep him!'

Andres shuddered. The very mention of the House of Laughter, a Chilean nickname for the secret headquarters of the CNI, filled every citizen of Santiago with dread.

'My father's got no information the CNI would want,' said Andres. 'So why take him to the torture?'

The caretaker shrugged. 'To those bastards, screams are

37

sweet music. Your Dad should know, shouldn't he?' He was referring to one of Juan's songs, banned by the Junta. It began:

> Do not feel sorry for the torturer
> He is happy in his work . . .

All the way to the National Stadium, Andres watched trucks pass him, crammed with prisoners. It was like match day, for the streets teamed with hundreds of people heading in the same direction, looking for someone—arrested in the night or gone missing.

There were hundreds more at the stadium, waiting outside a ring of troops; relatives, friends, neighbours, desperate for information. Please, Officer, can you . . .? My son, he . . . There must be some mistake . . . Will they announce the names? This food parcel, soldier, would it be possible to . . .?

'Back, back everybody!' ordered an officer. 'You know the score. Go to your homes!' Yes, the people of Santiago knew the score. It was a long time ago now, yet few would have forgotten the months and years of terror following the assassination of President Allende in the Moneda Palace— the mass arrests, the executions, the deaths in this very stadium.

They had come for Juan. They had beaten him up in the showers below the main stand. They had taken him for torture. They had kept him in a lightless cell for a year. Only Helen's persistence, supported by Horacio, Braulio and many friends—writing letters, making appeals, drawing up petitions—brought about Juan's release. Without being charged with any offence.

Now who've you got to help you, Juan? No Helen, no Horacio, no Braulio . . . Just me, against the generals. David versus Goliath. Andres managed a pale smile. Of course, David won, didn't he? His smile broadened. All I need is a sling and a well-aimed pebble.

He gazed at the weapons of the troops and his smile disappeared. Pebbles against machine-gun bullets . . .? Hm, Goliath may have lost, but all the Goliaths of this world who followed him learnt from his mistake—never fight fair.

Andres stayed clear of the crowd. He watched the arrival of another truck. The soldiers did not care if their brutality was witnessed by hundreds of people. Those prisoners who hesitated as they climbed from the truck were hastened on their way with rifle butts.

'Move, scum!'

Suddenly Andres broke forward, seeking a gap in the wall of people. 'Braulio!' There was no doubt. His friend had jumped from the truck. He was handcuffed. 'Braulio!' Andres fought to get through the crowd.

Braulio Altuna stood a head taller than the other prisoners in line. A stream of blood had congealed down one side of his face.

Andres forgot his own danger. He must get to Braulio, at the very least let him know that somebody had proof that he was alive.

'Please—please let me through—my friend is out there!' Andres looked to be having no luck in prising a way through the crowd when he spotted a tall man in a white mack, making better progress.

'Permiso! Give us a passage, folks—it's for a good cause.'

An American.

Andres tucked himself in behind the man, burly, fair-haired, with out-thrust arm, shoving a sideways path towards the truck and the gates of the stadium.

Andres got so close to the American that he could have picked his pocket. He glanced down and saw that the man was holding something behind him, wrapped in a carrier bag.

For an instant, Andres decided the American had a gun. Yet the compulsion to make contact with Braulio proved greater than Andres' fear that he might have landed himself in a shoot-out.

The object which the American slipped from the carrier bag had indeed many more shots than a pistol. A camera! He's a pressman. Andres felt a thrill of hope. Here comes the American cavalry! He was right behind the pressman. He shouted in Spanish:

'Give him room!' And then in a low voice only audible to the American: 'The world's got to know what's happening here.'

'You bet it has.' The pressman took Andres in in one friendly—even grateful—glance. They were comrades. Together they breasted a way through the crowd.

'That's my friend—the tall one.'

The last prisoners were being driven down from the truck. One was not fast enough to please his guards. He was hurt, hobbling, gripping his side in pain.

'Step on it, you red scab!'

The American's camera was in the air. A rifle butt swung against the stumbling prisoner.

Click-whirr, click-whirr—the scene was banked, recorded.

Braulio had turned, stepping out of line. He protested at the guard's action and immediately drew soldiers round him like wasps to honey.

Click-whirr, click-whirr. The toppling of Braulio was captured. Here was evidence for the time when villainy would be brought to justice.

Yet here also was terrible danger. The American photographer had himself been snapped by the eye of the officer commanding the troops. 'Christ, they've spotted me!' He lowered his camera swiftly below the shoulders of the crowd. He shifted, half-face, towards Andres. He seemed paralysed by fear.

The American pushed the camera into Andres' hand. 'Take this—I'm finished.'

'But—'

'I beg you. The film in that camera . . .'

The officer and his men were clubbing a passage through the crowd towards the American. Andres ducked the camera through the open zip of his jacket. 'Who shall I say?' He was being carried away from the pressman by the retreat of the crowd.

'Chailey—Don Chailey!' He yelled the name of his newspaper too but the words did not carry to Andres who found himself squeezed step by step away from the oncoming troops.

The crowd had saved Andres. It had no power to delay sentence upon the American. The soldiers were all round him. Momentarily his fair hair could be seen between their helmets. Then his arms went up above his head. He folded under a rampage of blows. He was hammered to the ground. He was kicked in the body, in the head, his hands stamped upon, his ribs skewered with iron-shod boots.

And now they were searching for his camera. They were demanding answers from the crowd, accusing them, turning their violence upon the innocent, frisking everyone who could have been within orbit of the American.

For an eternal second, Andres stood and watched. He saw Don Chailey dragged towards the stadium entrance. He saw him flung into one of the turnstiles.

Andres trembled as if touched by an electrified fence. Till now, he had wandered helplessly, insignificant. Soaked to the skin, he had arrived at the final blank wall and the closed gate. His brain, his heart, his passionate resolve—they were nothing in face of the Junta's untouchable strength.

But now . . . A chance in a million, an encounter lasting no longer than two minutes, had changed everything. He was in possession of something the military would like to get their hands on—proof of their brutality. What's more, Andres was witness to what the Black Berets had done to a citizen of the United States of America.

The Americans don't pour millions of dollars into Chile for us to beat up their newspapermen.

Andres was at the street corner, poised for flight. All at once he had a purpose, a direction, a next step. He tapped the camera reverently. Somehow I must contact the Resistance. What's in this camera might be just as valuable as bullets.

Three

Caution and common sense urged Andres to return to the mill and to his friends, Isa and Beto. Together they would decide what must be done with Don Chailey's photographs. Yet Andres was drawn, as if by a magnet, towards the little house in the Via Rivadivia which he and Juan had shared since the death of Helen.

He soothed the anxiety within him: I'll go soft as a whisper. Beto had warned him that the house would be watched by the secret police for Andres' return.

'You can spot a plain clothes man anywhere,' Andres had answered.

'And if they're holed up in the house opposite?'

'I'm not that important.'

As he reached the Via Rivadivia, he stepped back in shock. In his mind's eye he had expected to see the street as he remembered it—friendly and quiet, whitewashed, with the occasional balcony adorned with baskets of flowers; a sleepy street with blue-grey cobbles and trees casting tranquil shadows.

Instead, he witnessed a street under siege. Directly in front of him were a jeep and a military van. Beyond, in the centre of the street, a raging bonfire. He glanced up and saw blankets spread over window-sills like signal flags. There were at least ten soldiers on guard. Others were moving from one house to the next. So far there were no blankets hanging from the windows of Juan's house.

Our turn, I think. A crowd had gathered in the street and Andres had no difficulty concealing himself.

Weak sunshine had succeeded the rain, kindling steam from the pavements into a visual echo of smoke from the bonfire. Juan's bedroom window was thrown open. A second later—out came the books, the whole of Juan Larreta's library, and Andres' collection too, no doubt, hurtling through the sky, a rainstorm of knowledge, of ideas, of songs and poetry; flittering, soaring, smacking the pavement, sometimes shedding pages, sometimes falling as neatly as if placed there by a loving reader.

And the books were shovelled towards the bonfire.

Andres spied a few titles as they ploughed into one another on the ground: *The Eagle and the Serpent*, *War and Peace*, Neruda's poems, a biography of Mozart, the story of the Beatles, the drawings of William Blake, *Film Directors of Chile*, a life of Bolivar and, to Andres' momentary amusement, momentary grief—*Alice in Wonderland*, given him by his mother years and years ago.

Andres wanted to laugh. So the Junta is even afraid of *Alice in Wonderland*. One day I'll write a song about this: 'The Junta through the Looking Glass'. Yet he did not laugh. The scene before him of vicious and insane destruction was no laughing matter.

All Juan's songs in manuscript were being murdered.

The officer supervising the book-burning called to the crowd above the crackle of the bonfire. 'Thus, by order of the Junta, the property of all enemies of the state will be seized and destroyed.'

He paused for his words to sink in to the heads of his listeners. He watched the crowd whose eyes remained fixed upon the continuing avalanche of books, upon the flames, upon the pages curling, turning black, dissolving.

'The entertainer Juan Larreta was a traitor—to the nation, to the Holy Church and to the name of decency. The Interior Ministry has banned the publication of his work and the performance of his songs.'

The officer waited, as though half-expecting a backlash

of protest. Like the others, Andres silenced his opinion and saved his skin. Like the others, he felt cowed, ashamed, almost unclean.

He had listened to lies and he had not responded. He had not even whispered a protest.

The silence pleased the officer. He chose to interpret it as assent. Perhaps for a moment, in his heart, he had expected the crowd to defy him. Perhaps also in his heart he knew the lies he spoke. Yet he had won. He had declared injustice to be acceptable, and the crowd had let him get away with it.

Except, that is, for an old man at the rear of the crowd. He cried out, lonely, shrill, but courageous: 'Larreta was a good man. He spoke to the people's hearts.'

The old man's words were as petrol to the flames. 'Step forward—that man, step forward!'

The crowd was reluctant to open up for the old man. Andres recognised him. An Indian, who worked at the bakery down the road. Juan had sung at his grand-daughter's wedding.

He stood forward, bare-headed, in a suit that had grown old with him. He was bundled, without protest, without words, into the army van.

The officer delayed returning his pistol to its holster. He wagged it in the face of the crowd. 'Any more heroes?'

Andres' first comment as Isa unbarred the mill door to him was: 'I've got something to fight with!' He held up the camera. 'Not bullets, but evidence.'

Beto and Isa were also in a mood of burning anger. The laundry where Beto worked had been gutted by a fire-bomb. 'The rats've come out of their sewers,' he said. 'The vigilantes, doing their dirty-work under the protection of the army.'

Isa's school for under school-age children of working families had been closed down, by order of the police. The woman who ran the school had been taken in for questioning. 'And I just stood there. Like a dummy in a shop window. I feel ashamed. And guilty.'

'They'd have taken you too, Sis,' Beto soothed, 'if you'd said a single word. Right, Towny, what's in that camera of yours?'

'For one thing, a picture of my friend Braulio being beaten to a pulp outside the stadium. The rest—we'll have to find out.' Andres fished in his jacket pocket, still soaked from the storm, and took out a handbill printed on luminous yellow paper.

'Against your advice, I went home.' He unfolded the leaflet. 'This is all I've got left of Juan's possessions, and my own. Everything else, the troops burnt. In a very touching ceremony in front of the neighbours.' He smoothed out the leaflet.

Isa took it. 'Just the way they looked at the stadium.' The leaflet bore a photograph of Los Obstinados—Juan, Horacio and Braulio—and announced their recent northern tour to Antofagasta, Arica and across the border to La Paz and Lake Titicaca.

'They loved us in Peru,' said Andres wistfully. 'Juan was offered enough concerts for a year. But he came back to help the Silver Lion win the election.' He shrugged, half smiling. 'Horacio used to say, if Dad put money on a nag in a one-horse race it'd still come in last.'

The twins laughed. 'So?' Beto asked. 'How's this going to help?'

'Because it's printed by Horacio's cousin, Diego. The address of his printshop is on the bottom. He showed me round once. He's the only person I know who's got the equipment to develop and print these photos. What's more, they say he's a member of the old Resistance.'

Isa looked troubled. 'Then Security will be watching his place, round the clock.'

'The front, maybe,' agreed Andres. 'But you reach his

46

back door through a maze of passages. It's a risk, but it's better than hanging about at home waiting for old age.'

'After curfew, troops are shooting on sight,' reminded Isa.

'I've got to do something. Got to! I owe it to Juan and Braulio. And I owe it to Don Chailey . . .' He broke off. He stared at his friends. 'You think I'm sticking my nose into trouble again, don't you?'

The twins were getting used to him. They didn't chide him. Isa said, 'It'll be more than your nose in trouble if you don't change out of those wet clothes.'

'Where is this Diego's place?' Beto asked.

'Half an hour's walk.'

'Then first we eat,' Isa decided. 'We'll still have time to reach Diego's before curfew.'

'We? I'm not asking you two to risk your necks. Why should you?'

'That's not the sort of question to ask friends, Andres.' She pushed a towel into his hands. 'And perhaps because in future we've decided to share people's danger, rather than sit at home worrying what's happened to them.'

Beto grinned. He put on the drawl of an American movie cop: 'We want a slice of the action, Man.'

Nightfall, minutes after curfew. Three figures among dustbins to the rear of Diego Rosales' printshop. One of them at the door, lightly knocking.

Waiting, but no answer. Too dangerous to knock louder. Andres whispered to the others: 'Door's open.' His hand dropped to the latch. He pushed, and the scene was darkness.

Beto was beside Andres. 'Lock's been broken . . . the CNI?'

'Who else?' Andres was thinking, Diego at this moment might even be sharing a cell with Juan.

Isa was ahead of him. 'Let's look.' She edged the door

47

wider. It squeaked once, then lay silently back on its hinges.

'See anything?'

'Not yet. But I can *feel* what they've done.'

The place was a ruin. The street-side window gave enough light to outline the scene of devastation. In the centre of the room stood the shattered hulk of an offset litho printing machine. The type founts which lined the room had been ripped from the walls and hurled in all directions. There were mounds of paper, burned; furniture, smashed; ink-tubes daubed on every surface.

'They must have used sledgehammers.'

'Pick-axes, actually.' The voice stunned the intruders. It came from below ground.

'Diego?'

'What's left of me.' Horacio's cousin climbed achingly up the basement steps. He held a torch muzzled by an old sock.

'Andres Larreta, Diego—do you remember me?'

The printer straightened up from the steps. He grasped Andres' hand and shook it warmly. 'I didn't think they made ghosts so solid these days. *The Mercury* said—'

Andres interrupted to quell Diego's rising hopes. 'The CNI. They shot Horacio. They snatched Juan . . . I'm sorry.'

'And yet you—'

'He's the cat with nine lives,' smiled Isa. She held out her hand. 'This is Beto. I'm Isabel.'

'Twins, eh?'

'My bodyguards,' said Andres.

Diego sighed. 'That's what I could have done with.' He glanced about him. 'As you can see, my guests didn't stay for supper.'

They all laughed: true Chileans, making light of despair.

'What can I do for you folks—print you a poem of praise to the Junta, one line long?' As he shuffled towards his press, Isa and Beto noticed how crippled he was, that his spine seemed locked, forcing him to move at an angle, dragging his left foot a little. He felt their eyes on him. 'I walk like this to scare off the crows.'

Yet Andres knew: Diego had been imprisoned and tortured after the overthrow of President Allende by the generals. His spinal cord had been permanently damaged. But not his spirit; not his humour.

'We brought you this.' Andres took Don Chailey's camera from a plastic carrier bag. 'I got it from a Yankee photographer before the Black Berets dragged him into the stadium. He's probably dead by now.'

Diego turned the Nikon SLR camera over in his hand. 'Expensive. Not used for taking wedding snapshots.'

'There's a picture of Braulio Altuna. He was one of the prisoners. They were beating him and . . . well, it's all there—evidence.'

'He handed you the camera—just like that?'

'He'd no alternative. Anyway, we'd become friends.' Andres paused but nobody challenged him. 'Who knows what else could be on that film?'

In the pale amber light Diego's eyes shone with excitement. He held up the camera. 'I have an instinct, a feeling. Fact is, friends, I'm getting—vibrations!'

Isa indicated the carnage left by the CNI hurricane. 'Aren't you in enough trouble, Diego?'

'I'm clean,' Diego replied chirpily. 'They found nothing. Because I believed this election was a fraud from the start. Too good to be true. Zuckerman and his brother butchers agreed to it simply to persuade the democrats to come out of the woodwork. Now they're being picked off by the thousand.'

'But your equipment?'

'I've stuff hidden all over the city.' Diego tapped his nose with his forefinger. 'Come downstairs.'

The CNI had not spared Diego's basement in their search for evidence against him. 'Just occasionally fate deals you a little bit of luck.'

'You call this luck?' exclaimed Beto. 'It's worse than upstairs.'

'True, those boys tried hard. Ripped out my phone. Overturned my stove. Smashed my fridge. Stole all my spaghetti. But when it came to the pinch—gallant. Look!' Diego pointed to two adjacent doors, stencilled in white letters: GENTLEMEN and LADIES. 'They trampled over everything, but they stayed out of the Ladies.'

Diego hobbled forward. He pushed open the door marked LADIES to reveal his photographic dark-room, its equipment intact. His moustache quivered above an ear-to-ear grin. 'Long live the Resistance!'

Don Chailey's photographs were to prove even more sensational in content than Andres, Diego and the twins could have imagined. 'Andres, you've struck a gusher,' was Diego's first amazed response. He had been examining the developed film with a magnifying glass. 'We've got something here that could rock Zuckerman and the Junta back on their Nazi heels.'

To enable the others to see the photo frames, Diego slipped the head of the film into the projection device on his enlarger. He switched on the enlarger light, at the same time turning off the dark-room light. All that could be seen now, in eerie negative, was what Don Chailey had witnessed through the lens of his camera.

The first picture was a telephoto shot of the Silver Lion, Miguel Alberti, on the speakers' platform at the stadium. Behind him were election placards and a sea of faces. The next picture focused down on one face in particular— swarthy, black moustached, unsmiling among those round about him who were cheering and waving.

'Mr X, I presume.'

The next picture jolted Andres to the heart. It was of Juan, and at each side of him, Horacio and Braulio, mouths wide in chorus. Juan's craggy face beamed with spiritedness and relish for the song and the vast crowd's response.

'I'll make you a copy of that, Andres,' offered Diego.

'There's that face again,' said Isa. 'What's he holding?'

'Looks like a walkie-talkie,' thought Beto.

Diego hesitated before moving on to the next picture. 'Now this one will take your breath away.'

The photograph showed the murder of Miguel Alberti in the market place at San José. The Silver Lion had stretched out his hand to the crowd. He had suddenly flicked back his head. Don Chailey had pressed the shutter at the instant the assassin's bullet struck Miguel's throat.

'My God!'

Diego's whisper came hoarse and almost inaudible. 'His murder. And look—his murderer!'

The man with the walkie-talkie. Captured in profile. Slightly blurred, yet unmistakably holding a revolver.

'That man's Security. No question,' insisted Beto.

'No question,' echoed Diego.

'Then . . .' Isa looked closer at the murder scene, at the murder weapon fitted with a silencer. 'Then the Junta killed the Silver Lion.'

Andres could not take his eyes off the face of the murderer. Could this also be the commander of the Security men who had snatched Juan away? There was a resemblance. 'So the Junta puts the blame on the Communists . . . Which gives them the excuse to, to . . .' He felt sick with grief.

Diego's hand rested comfortingly on his shoulder. 'To pull the chain on all their enemies.'

'For just seeing these pictures,' said Isa, 'they'd kill us.'

Diego chuckled and broke the tension. 'If that's the case, what punishment do you think they'd dream up for the poor idiot who published the pictures?'

Don Chailey's next photo zoomed in on the assassin, revealing him in full face, and capturing, for the last fleeting instant, the barrel of his gun.

Evidence.

The camera had pursued him, trapped him in its lens again and again. It spied him beating a way through the stunned crowd. It snapped him so close that the stitch marks of a neck wound were plainly visible.

'Reach me the firewater, Beto,' requested Diego. 'My head's like a ten-pin bowling alley.' He uncorked the half-drunk bottle of Aguardente and took a gulp. 'I mean, if these pictures got on to the front pages of the world's press!' He handed the bottle round. 'Of course, only a man who'd taken complete leave of his senses would process this stuff. Huh, only a chump who thought the House of Laughter was a joke shop on the Alameda.'

The last of Chailey's photographs were of army activity: arrests in the street; the battering open of doors; a woman struck attempting to prevent soldiers taking her son away; a man discovered hiding behind wooden barrels—and the soldiers pushing the barrels on top of him.

And, of course, the attack upon Braulio.

'Talking of damn-fool heroes, this Yankee was one. He must have been crazy, taking such risks. And for what? For glory?'

'For the truth, maybe,' said Isa. 'Because he saw injustice.'

Diego took another swig of the firewater. 'He'll get no thanks for his bravery.' His face was bitter and furious. 'Today the shops were open as usual, doing a roaring business. Who cares?'

Andres had no doubts. 'You do, Diego. And we do too.'

'Four of us among a million . . . Perhaps ten, fifteen if we count absent friends.'

'There are thousands of Chileans who'd salute Don Chailey for what he did.'

'But how many would stand by him in his hour of need, eh?' Diego stared hard, searchingly, at his friends. He read their thoughts, their resolution. 'You lot are as crazy as the

Yankee. You're standing there—I can see it in your eyes, and you're queuing up for the Pendura. You actually want to be tortured!'

He wrested the bottle from Beto, to whom he had only just passed it. He emptied it with a huge gulp. And all at once, he was calm. 'You want to help? Okay, but understand this—there's no going back.' He paused. He glanced from face to face. 'Are you in this together?'

'No,' answered Andres. 'Just me. Isa and Beto have risked enough already on my behalf.'

'We're in!' Beto's tone brooked no contradiction. 'Our own parents—they disappeared too. We're sick of waiting.'

Diego was now quite relaxed. 'Very well. The long and the short of it is that I need a printing press.'

'And we've transport,' said Isa.

'Excellent. Then all I ask is for you three to do a spot of fetching and carrying for me. If I take one step outside this place, I'll have two pistol-packing shadows wherever I go.'

Diego explained that, immediately the elections had been announced, he had decided to dismantle the smallest of his three printing presses. He had wrapped up each part and taken the pieces to friends and acquaintances—but only those who had never been in trouble before with the police or Security.

'Trusties, if you like. People who live such quiet lives that the CNI don't know they exist. But friends of a free Chile all the same.'

'You want us to call on them,' Beto asked, 'pick up the parts?'

'Not exactly, though the plan I have in mind is just as risky.' He coughed. 'For you, that is.' Diego assured the three volunteers that if they did not care for his plan, there would be no bad feeling if they decided not to go ahead with it.

'It's brazen—and that's why it could succeed.' He smiled,

almost cheekily. 'All you'll be needing is a cool head, lots of luck—and . . .' He leaned forward with exaggerated secrecy. 'And a porter's uniform.'

Four

In the stadium of Santiago the number of prisoners has reached six thousand and there are new arrivals every hour. For each lorry load there is an official reception: prisoners are ordered along a corridor beneath the main stand. This corridor is lined with troops—the Black Berets, who beat the prisoners with their rifles. A broken arm, a smashed elbow—these are a small price to pay for avoiding a shattered skull.

Those who fall are kicked and beaten. They crawl and they are kicked and beaten again. For the wounded there are no doctors. For those who die under the onslaught, there are the baths where their bodies are stacked until other soldiers detailed for the task cart them away.

The guards in the stadium are as tense, as trigger-happy, as the prisoners are afraid. Even a stare, a suspicious movement, earns a blow from rifle butt or truncheon.

The prisoners face death as sudden as a precipice. And the step before the precipice is madness—that same fear people experience when an enemy within threatens to hurl them over the edge against their will.

Such an impulse has gripped a prisoner in the upper level of the stand. He has cupped his face in his hands. His voice shrieks out across the stadium: 'Death to the Fascist murderers!'

All eyes find the man. All eyes see him climb the rail, high, giddy, towering above the slopes of tiered concrete below. All eyes see the man launch himself into space.

Though his body does not move on landing, the Black

Berets take no chances. They batter him. They drag him. They curse at his death as if somehow they feel cheated by him. The Commandant waits at the entrance to the grandstand tunnel. He shoots the dying protester in the head.

'Down with Fascism!'

It is unbelievable. Amid such terror, witnessing brutal death, yet another man has volunteered for his own execution.

'Who was that?'

The stadium listens.

The man stands up. 'I did.'

'Come over here!'

Calmly, slowly, the prisoner walks towards the Commandant.

On the stroke of midday at the Central Station of Santiago, a young porter in a peaked cap and ill-fitting uniform rose from checking a wheel on his empty parcel trolley. He looked about him, his heart thumping.

The north-facing concourse of the station was, as usual, packed with crowds arriving and departing. The only sign of martial law was a bored soldier, machine-gun over his shoulder, pacing unhurriedly between the ticket counters at one side of the entrance and the left-luggage lockers at the other.

Andres and the twins had waited three days—three happy, peaceful days together—before Diego's signal for action came: 'It's on. Friday. Prompt at twelve.'

Andres could see, at an angle, the outside of the station. There, in spring-white sunshine, wagged the tufted orange head of Orlando the Ostrich, one of the star performers of the Marionetas de los Gemelos.

A small audience had gathered to watch Isa as she deftly controlled the puppet and at the same time played a tune on a mouth organ. Her green panama lay upside down on the pavement, inviting contributions.

Beyond the queue at the taxi rank were two policemen, in olive uniforms. They were chatting to each other but also watching Isa and Orlando. One of them crossed the forecourt, rather more compelled by Isa's beauty than the capers of the dancing ostrich.

Andres bit his lip: he's going to move her on. Beto had been right, so much could go wrong with this plan of Diego's. Yet they were committed. There was no retreat. He checked through the plan again in his head: Diego's friends had all been successfully contacted. They would bring the parts of the printing press and leave them in the left-luggage lockers, then cross the forecourt and drop the keys to the lockers into Isa's panama. 'Plus a little cash!'

Andres' job was to retrieve the keys and, protected by his official porter's uniform, unlock the mystery items, place them on the trolley and then wheel them out of the station.

Beto would be waiting in the van to load up. Isa would join Beto and Andres—and they would drive away.

Simple!

And crazy, Andres was beginning to think.

Orlando was causing laughter in the crowd by letting his long neck and head follow the notes of the mouth organ— sweeping the pavement with his beak on the low notes, reaching for the Andes on the high notes. Even the policeman smiled.

Andres' eye was diverted to the lockers. A woman, calm, inserting a shopping bag into the locker, turning, looking to neither right nor left, moving towards the arc of sunlight and into the crowd of spectators.

The policeman still watched Orlando's performance. He chuckled as Orlando thrust out a red, skinny leg to a small child who shook his foot vigorously and laughed with delight. The woman waited, then she crossed in front of the crowd, dropping something into the panama.

Somebody else at the lockers. A middle-aged man, short, very nervous, locking away a small suitcase, putting his hand to his head, wiping away sweat—and suddenly spying the soldier; on the verge of panic.

Go on, go on, urged Andres silently. Do it! The man looked so flustered and so guilty that for an instant it seemed as if he might rush to the policeman and beg to be arrested. He edged forward into the crowd. He immediately got his shoes pecked by Orlando.

Pesos fell into the green panama—and something else.

Two down, five to go. 'Thanks . . . and good luck!' Isa said, resting her mouth organ for a moment.

'Here, you! Porter!'

Andres almost jumped out of his skin. 'M-me?'

'Yes, you—porter!' It was the soldier. He had spotted two attractive fashionably dressed girls step from a taxi. They each carried a heavy suitcase. The soldier's boredom had vanished. There was a swagger in his step. 'Help these lovely señoritas with their luggage, sonny.'

'Me—but!'

'If you don't want my boot up your ass—snap to it!'

'I've to look after . . . my trolley, Officer.'

The soldier was too flushed with the smiles of the girls to tolerate excuses. He piled their cases on to Andres' trolley. 'Which platform, my beauties?'

The girls were as frightened of the soldier as Andres was. 'Nine, I think.'

'Then nine it is.'

Andres had no choice: he must obey. If he was a porter, then he must port. He sighed. He would have liked Isa to see what was happening, but her back was turned; and there was another figure at the lockers.

He almost pushed his trolley into the shins of a station supervisor. 'Sorry, Sir.'

The supervisor stepped aside. His thoughts were elsewhere, yet he glanced at Andres. And the glance became a stare. 'You the new one?'

Andres felt himself choking on his own saliva. He nodded. 'New—yes.'

'See me directly you've finished this job.

'Well, I—'

'Directly!'

Andres nodded. He gulped for breath. H thought that he had got away. 'What are you doing with that?'

'Doing?'

'With the trolley . . . Leave it. Leave it and carry the cases.'

Platform nine. These cases were heavier than barrelfuls of water. What've you got in here, ladies—machine-guns? An anti-tank gun? All I need now is a slipped disc.

'Here, Señor,' called one of the girls just as Andres was beginning to think they had booked seats on the engine itself. 'Compartment A, Seats 18 and 19, por favor!'

There was an elderly lady already in the compartment. She was reading General Zuckerman's speech to the nation printed in bold type on the front page of *The Mercury*, tracing each line with her forefinger.

'Excuse me, Señora.' Twice Andres tried to lift one of the cases on to the luggage rack. The second time brought him, off balance, right down into *The Mercury* and the General's fine words. 'Terribly, terribly—'

'You oaf!'

'So sorry—I'm new.' He tried again with the case and succeeded. The second rattled metallically as he heaved it on to the rack. He looked at the girls. He smiled. 'Sounds like you've got the kitchen stove in there.'

'Presents,' was the reply. One of the girls thrust a tip into Andres' hand. 'Muchas gracias!'

'De nada.'

'Young man.' The elderly lady was holding out a hundred pesos note. 'Fetch me a coffee, if you please.' She pointed across to the next platform where there was a mobile drinks stall.

'But Señora—'

'Don't "but" me . . . just slip over there and fetch the coffee—black, with a level teaspoonful of sugar.'

Andres willed himself to be firm. 'That's platform eight, Señora. My territory's platform nine and I'm not permitted to cross the tracks.'

'Young man—you get that coffee this instant or I will complain to the guard.'

He took the money. He could ill-afford to argue or to answer complaints. He decided he would go and simply not return. He went out into the corridor. At the open carriage door he slipped off his peaked cap and peered out. He jerked his head in again swiftly.

The supervisor was pounding down the platform—and with him were a policeman and an officer of the Black Berets. Andres crossed the corridor. Platform eight was empty: it was his only way. He pushed down the window. From the outside he twisted the door handle. Locked!

Hearing Andres' efforts, the elderly lady had come half way down the corridor. 'What's keeping you, boy?'

'The door, Señora—somebody's left it locked.'

'Then use your wits. Climb out of the window—see, he's taking his stall away!'

'This is highly irregular, Señora. But if you insist.'

'I do insist!'

Andres obeyed. He cocked his leg out of the window. He lowered his head and shunted himself forward. 'Hell!' A train was coming in to platform eight. It shimmered in an arcade of steel and light. Andres dropped on to the track. The train was slowing. He could hear the squeal of breaks. 'Huh, the things people ask porters to do!'

He hopped over the rails and, from the safety of the platform, watched the train pass where he had stood seconds before. Was it milk and no sugar she wanted, or sugar and no milk? The train blocked the old lady's view of that inept young man who was striding clean past the drinks stall with the hundred pesos note still clutched in his hand.

The ticket collector did not give Andres a second glance—and there was the trolley waiting patiently for him. I've two minutes if I'm lucky before the supervisor blows the whistle on me. Andres touched his cap to the bored soldier as he wheeled the trolley across the vast concourse towards the lockers. He paused. He looked out into the sunlight.

Bless her! Isa had not shifted from her post.

Time to make a move.

The new performer is Silvestro, a gangly, skull-grinning skeleton whose head emits a comical shriek as it springs up from wobbling shoulders.

'You want change, Señor?' Isa asks as Andres approaches, displaying his hundred pesos note. Andres nods. He closes out the light as he stoops towards the panama. There are hands, two bodies, a shift of movement. Keys end up in Andres' left hand. With his right he drops the note into the Panama. 'Muchas gracias.'

'My pleasure!'

The instant Andres turns towards the lockers, Isa brings her show to a close. There is applause, a rain of pesos into the panama. She empties it. She spins her puppets round on their strings, rolls up the controls and replaces Orlando and Silvestro in her case. She walks with the case to the edge of the pavement. She goes left past the queue for the taxis.

Andres has opened the first locker. He recovers the parcel and lays it, with desperate calm, on the trolley. The second key proves difficult. Come on, blast you! Then he realises he is trying to insert it upside down. Idiot. Oaf. The old woman was right.

The locker door swings open. Large, awkward parcel, this; and heavy. Labelled, WITH GREAT CARE. On to the trolley. Next locker—a canvas holdall, containing several items. Heavy as the girls' cases. Rattling a bit, too.

'Keeping you busy, are they?' It is the nosy soldier, right behind Andres.

'Always busy.' He has to decide—to stop and talk or to carry on. He goes to the next locker, opens it. Just a small parcel, but of an odd shape.

'Overstayed, have they?'

'Overstayed?'

'Well, gone over their time.'

'Oh yes, yes.'

'What happens if nobody comes to claim them?'

Locker number five—an item so small it hardly seemed to be worth leaving in such a spacious cubicle. 'My job's just to—'

'Anybody check out the content of these things?'

'Oh yes.' Andres is running with sweat. He drags at his collar. He half turns. He wants to remind the soldier that there are plenty of better things a sentry can do with his time than spend it chatting to a junior porter.

He is to be spared more of the soldier's breath on his neck: a black van screeches into the station forecourt. 'Here's trouble—our pals the arm-twisters.' Clearly the soldier doesn't care for the Security any more than Andres does.

The rear doors of the van open. Three plain-clothes men descend. At the same moment, the officer of the Black Berets strides out through the gate of platform nine. Two policemen follow him, escorting the girls Andres helped only minutes ago.

The girls are handcuffed.

'What a waste!' mutters the soldier. 'There'll be no lipstick or high-heels where they're being taken.'

Behind the prisoners comes the station supervisor. Andres opens locker number seven. The parcel seems to contain rollers. He adds it to his pile. He feels on his back the distant yet burning gaze of the supervisor.

As the girls are bundled violently into the Security van,

the supervisor calls to Andres. 'You—porter!' The voice cuts through a station announcement of the departure of the train from platform nine. Whoever expects to greet the girls off the train at Valdivia will wait a long, long time.

'You're wanted,' calls the soldier. 'The gaffer.'

Andres surveys his route to freedom. Thirty paces into sunlight, then left past the taxi rank. He surveys the route to captivity. He sees also a surge of passengers coming out from platform ten, crossing the path—and the vision—of the station supervisor.

It's got to be now.

A family, borne down with luggage, passes between Andres and the soldier. He begins to move. He wheels the trolley, his back to everything, his face leaning towards the sun.

He hears the shouts. But there are announcements. He feels the rush of people between him and the supervisor. He does not look round. He is pushing the trolley as though he is in a pram race with a prize of a fortnight's holiday in Disneyland. He is out, on the pavement, passing the swelling queue for the taxis. Pushing, steering, watching his cargo and the way ahead, till he is at the station corner.

Come on, Beto—come on!

Beto's van is stuck at the traffic lights, waiting for a right filter into the station forecourt. He has already picked up Isa. He sees Andres and the trolley.

The girls have been locked in the black van. Their cases are guarded by two policemen. The officer of the Black Berets has his arms folded. Apparently he refuses to give up the cases to the Security. Protocol!

The station supervisor has his hands on his hips at the station entrance. And on his mind is the young porter who has disappeared with railway property. He looks right and left. He does not see Andres. He turns right. He walks a few paces. He stops. He changes course, brooding, getting angry.

63

The lights change for Beto. Isa squats next to the rear doors of the van, ready to fling them open.

Come on, Beto—come on!

The supervisor is striding left now, past the taxi rank. He pauses. He glances towards the line of traffic crossing the square.

Beto brakes hard. The doors open. Isa is out, helping with the parcels. 'Well done, Towny!' cries Beto.

'I think I'm being followed.'

Arms now folded, the supervisor is baffled. No trolley. No porter. Not to be beaten, he continues towards the station corner.

'That's the lot.' Isa and Andres leap aboard, Isa pulling the van doors to. 'Move!'

Beto needs no prompting. He is accelerating towards a gap in the traffic. The supervisor has walked several paces further. He is about to give up and return the way he came when he sees the empty trolley.

'Well I'll be . . .' The sun is in his eyes. He shades them. He stares out.

'That's him!' cries Andres, ducking.

'Did he see us?'

Andres slumps into the back of the van. 'Any more of this and I'll need a heart transplant.'

Such was Beto's joy at their success that, as he pulled out into the fast traffic of the Alameda, he burst into song. And it was a Juan Larreta song:

> 'Over this dry-sweet land
> My body lies scattered
> My head in the desert
> My feet in the southern snows
> My eyes in the castles
> Of the blood-red sky.

Andres approved. He would have joined in had he not

been struggling out of the porter's uniform into his own clothes.

Isa, however, was staring at the wing-mirror of the van. 'Don't count your chickens,' she said eventually. 'I think we're being tailed.'

'Oh no!'

'That breakdown truck.'

The Alameda was carrying them east, with the great hill of San Cristóbal on their left.

'I'll turn off. See if they stay with us.'

Andres kept his head down. A tide of fear washed coldly through him. Things had been going too well. But he wasn't going to upset the driver. He must spend the next moments thinking ahead.

Beto braked smoothly. He signalled a right turn into a busy shopping street. He groaned. 'No luck—they're right behind . . . Isa, what do we do?'

Isa stayed calm. 'Don't speed up, that's for sure. They don't seem in any hurry, so relax.'

'Relax?'

'Now bear left.'

'Still with us?' asked Andres, hoping for good news.

'Right up our backsides! Hell we're in a jam.'

'How many of them?'

'Two. Thinking of taking them on?'

'Listen,' said Isa. 'Either they saw us put the stuff on board and plan to track us to our destination—'

'Or?'

'They're following us because they've nothing better to do.'

Beto was almost in a fever, glancing so much in his rear mirror that he was ignoring the traffic in front of him. He braked hard, a whisker away from a collision. 'Y'see? We're trapped.'

'I can think of one thing we can do,' said Andres. 'To save the printing press.'

'Save the press?' howled Beto. 'It's us we've got to save!'

'We can do both.' Andres' confidence pacified Beto. He stayed silent. 'I know one place . . . We might just shake them off long enough to get rid of the cargo.'

'Okay, Towny. Your wish is my command.'

Andres instructed Beto to head south and west. 'The town drops away and there are fir woods.'

Isa nodded, recognising the location which Andres described. 'Hills and bends—it's a chance.'

Beto forgot his own fear as he listened to Andres' plan. 'So at these fir woods, I speed up, win some distance. When our friends are out of sight, we stop, you take the press in the sacks and do a vanishing trick into the trees.'

'And you two carry on. Do your puppet show as usual.'

'We'll come back for you later,' said Isa.

'No. I'll hide the stuff. Then I'll make my own way back to the mill.'

'It's a devil of a distance. You'd not make it before curfew.'

'I'll be careful.'

Isa had a better idea. 'There's a refuge we know, less than an hour from the woods.' She described the route to the Seminary of Our Lady of Mercy. 'Ask for Father Mariano, and just mention our names.'

Andres smiled widely. 'Bed and breakfast in a seminary—say no more!'

The Security truck continued to follow Beto at a leisurely pace. At the outskirts of the city, the roads were almost empty, except for the occasional fast car heading west to the hills and the ocean.

Isa slipped into the rear of the van and helped Andres pack the various sections of the printing press into two tough sacks.

'We're getting close to the spiral road, Beto,' warned Andres. 'In a couple of kilometres there's a right bend into the trees. Then the road dips and twists.'

Beto eased his foot down on the accelerator. The distance between van and truck increased slowly. The truck did not accelerate: what did it matter so long as the van was in sight?

The trees had arrived, and the sharp right bend. 'Now!' shouted Beto giving himself the starting order. He rammed the accelerator to the ground.

'How far, Andres?' asked Isa.

'Next bend.'

'Next bend it is, comrades!' cried Beto, hunched in excitement over the steering wheel. 'Then all brakes go.' The next corkscrew bend whipped up into the van's face. 'They're nowhere!'

Andres had fixed himself against the roof and sides of the van. He might never see Isa and Beto again. That, rather than the danger ahead of him, seized his thoughts.

'It's now, Towny!'

An almighty shudder rocked the van as Beto chose his landing ground. For an instant the van threatened to career right over the edge of the road. Yet the brakes held, bringing the vehicle to a lurching standstill on the hard shoulder next to the trees. 'Away you go!'

Andres pushed open the rear doors. He jumped out, followed by Isa. They dragged the sacks, clanking, on to their shoulders. They were in among the trees, out of view of the road.

'Take care, caro!' She kissed him. He watched her dart from shadows into soft afternoon sunlight. She waved. He saw her face as she pulled the van doors to, as Beto zoomed out into the road again.

Getting a kiss like that was worth the risk. He touched the spot. 'Bless you, Isa!' He moved in a flicker of shadows, humping one sack, dragging the other. He stopped. He could hear the Security truck. In no hurry—that's good. He took extra cover behind a tree trunk. He watched the truck pass.

From the occupants, not a sideways glance.

Some detectives! There must have been tyre marks on the road, yet the driver never looked beyond his elbow. Go to the bottom of the class.

Andres was not prepared to chance the sanctuary of only five lanes of pine. He crouched. He drove himself forward through the trees, head lowered. Then without warning, without hint or gasp, there was an empty space beneath him.

His hands let go the sacks at the instant of falling. He reached out. At nothing. For there was nothing, except feeble tree-growths extending from the sheer wall of sand-stone.

He fell. Fast enough and far enough to knock himself cold among tree roots and a scree of red shale.

'Petrol's running low,' grumbled Beto as the van approached Puente Alto.

'The school's just up the hill and off to the left. Another five minutes and the kids'll be out.'

Beto sighed. 'I wonder if the CNI like puppets.' He slowed, he turned. 'Look, Sis, if they arrest us—'

'If they arrest us, we never mention Andres.'

'I'll try to remember that as they're sticking the electrodes all over me.'

'And you never believe them if they tell you that I've confessed. It's a trick they play.'

They were approaching the main gates of the school of San Bernardo. 'Let's change the conversation, shall we? I'm going hot and cold already.'

The Security truck had also steered across traffic into the quiet road of San Bernardo; quiet that is, until the school bell struck.

Isa smiled. She glanced in the mirror at their pursuers. 'Saved by the bell!'

'For the present.'

The school children were hurtling out into the playground. As the first of them reached the gates they were met by the sound of the quena and of Silvestro the Skeleton doing a wild dance on the pavement.

'Welcome to the Marionetas de los Gemelos, friends!' shouted Beto. 'The finest puppets in South America! Famous throughout the world and beyond!'

If the Security had planned an arrest, they would have to postpone it, for the whole school, it seemed, was now surrounding the Marionettes of the Twins, clapping hands to Isa's tune.

In the cab of the Security truck, the driver's fingers moved on the steering wheel, following the beat. His partner also nodded to the rhythm.

Neither of them realised that the tune they were enjoying so much was written by Juan Larreta, one of the Disappeared.

The son of Juan Larreta awoke without a tune in his head, but with a view of his toes protruding from his shoe like a hot-dog from its bread. He raised his body on one elbow, looking for ketchup. He did not feel broken.

When he was eleven he had fallen out of a juniper tree trying to rescue his friend Costas' pet monkey, Don Quixote. It was then he had learnt what a broken bone actually felt like. These were just bruises, skin ruptures where rock and shale had gone for him like those two full-backs in his trial for Chago youth.

He was alive and he was grateful. He gazed up at the point where he had become aviator without wings. He felt his head. Isa's plaster over his wound was still intact.

Miracles do happen. He moved himself. Nothing serious, merely a jab of pain as he reached sitting position. I must have been out for the count for ages. It's getting dark. I've to shift myself. But I need a bit more rest.

The hideaway was worth remembering. The wall behind

69

Andres continued on two sides. The ground was covered with scrub. On the fourth side of this amiable prison there was a slope guarded by tall red willows.

He examined the rock above him. Beneath an overhanging tree stump, prickly with new outgrowths, there was an arch of rock. Here some animal had scooped out a home for itself. I could hide the press in there. Come back for it later.

Andres stood up. He brushed himself off. He tried walking, five steps forward, turn, five steps back. Painful, but he was all right.

He climbed the easy route to the top of the rock wall and, almost without parting the grass, retrieved the sacks from the quarry edge.

The main thing is to be able to remember this spot again.

He went through the trees towards the road. Easy—a sign warning drivers of the dangerous bend ahead. He measured the distance with his eye. Thirty paces.

He returned to the rock face and the overhang. Using a sharp stone Andres dug the existing hole deeper and wider. Mustn't leave this lot for long or it'll go rusty. He buried the sacks. He covered them over with shale. He stood back, balancing on his toes.

Andres' thoughts returned to his father, Juan, and his brief good cheer faded. Am I doing this for you, Dad, and all the others . . .? Or just to keep you out of my mind?

He was about to climb back to the upper ground when suddenly wood pigeons burst out of the top branches of the firs.

Something coming.

Andres heard trucks. They had turned off the main road. They were close. He dived to earth. He could almost feel the trucks through the thin partition of trees. They were moving down, in a semi-circle, roaring in first gear.

And I thought I was in the middle of nowhere. He could see the track now, a route of mud twisting and descending steeply. Army trucks!

Andres knew that he must put distance between him and the hiding place. If he was to be caught, it mustn't be here. He came down the bank of shale. He crossed through the trees. A thick passageway of firs opened downwards into a quarry.

What can they want down there?

He followed, softly over beds of pine needles, then stopped where the trees did. Reflecting the darkening sky was a wide pool in the quarry bottom.

Prisoners.

There were two trucks. They had halted where the mud track skirted the pool. The prisoners were being ordered down at gun point and made to line up along the edge of the water.

At first Andres thought the prisoners might have been brought here to do forced labour, to dig shale, perhaps, or break rocks, as happened in films. He refused to consider the alternative—the thing soldiers did in real life in quarries hidden away from the eyes of the world.

The prisoners were made to face the water.

No!

In seconds, it happened: three soldiers with machine-guns, firing from the hip. A burst of a few moments long, sending terrified birds soaring up and away, catching the last rays of the sun on their feverish wings.

The prisoners were dead. And the quarry was silent.

Five

The machine-gun fire echoed in Andres' brain. The shock exploded in his stomach. He could not keep still, yet his legs would not hold him. He saw the dying. He saw them as they fell; some where they stood, like slow-sliding rocks; some hurled into death like doors smashed from their hinges.

Andres has seen his mother die, and all the grief of that moment came back, shaking him till his teeth chattered.

I . . .

He would not close his eyes. He would not turn away. He owed it to the dead. He owed it to her, to them.

I am a witness.

He watched the finishing-off. He watched the officer go from body to body. Where there was movement, a tremor—one shot.

Thirty men: living souls despatched into air, without memory, without record. Just thirty more to add to the list of the Disappeared. Thirty corpses rolled into the shallow grave of water.

Persons Unknown.

Andres watched the soldiers climb aboard the trucks. He felt freezing cold, as though his blood had been drained from him. He watched the trucks come up the mud track towards him. He was not exposed, but he was close. Yet he did not move. He was ice. He saw the soldiers smoking. He saw their faces. He saw no meaning.

For minutes he did not move. Only his brain functioned. To die so suddenly. Not even to be granted a last cigarette, a prayer. To be sent into the darkness while out there, on the fashionable boulevards of Santiago, the cash tills rang merrily and martinis were served at pavement cafes in the balmy spring air.

A toast to the Junta.

To the saviours of the nation.

General Zuckerman is God.

God's in the presidential palace.

And all's right with the world.

Andres' first instinct was to run, to escape the presence of the forlorn dead. He could do nothing for them. Yet he stayed. The breeze discovered tears in his eyes. It made them drop on to his cheeks.

Run, little boy, said the breeze. And keep your mouth shut about all this. These men no longer matter: they did not exist.

Andres spoke out loud: 'Adiós, little boy!'

You are going down.

I am a man.

You are going down?

I must know.

You are a fool.

I am a witness. And I have a father. I must go down.

The road wound in a sharp loop but Andres cut straight across a bank of muddy reeds. He ignored the warning thought that the soldiers might have posted a guard at the top of the track. Too bad. I'm committed.

He slowed, momentarily afraid of approaching the bodies. I must. He stopped. Got to! What are you scared of—that they'll grab you by the ankle?

I will count the bodies and if I can discover their names . . . Move! Go closer. Touch them.

No!

Then how will you ever see their faces?

The water was at Andres' feet. Its coldness grabbed his ankles, not the fingers of the dead.

Eyes open—move!

73

This first body had been carried two metres backwards by the force of the bullets and half-floated in the water. Andres bent towards it. His hand sought a hold on the shoulder. He let go.

You can—you must!

He pulled the body against his legs. He heaved it over and water fell from the face.

Not Juan.

Search him. Andres unbuttoned a short cotton jacket. He felt for the inside pocket. There was nothing. He reached for the dead man's hand. One ring—that's all.

Tug it off.

That's theft.

It's identification: see, initials.

He pulled at the ring. He depressed the skin of the finger, swollen around the gold. 'Come off, damn you!'

Obediently, the corpse released its identity.

All at once, Andres was filled with anger—at himself. Why are you doing this? Why are you lumbering yourself? All that matters is to learn if Juan is among the dead.

If not, let the dead bury their dead.

He cursed himself, but still went from body to body as though each one meant something to him, as though each one had been a friend.

And the heads turned, and the faces turned, and the water streamed from their dead hair and from their closed eyes; and their limbs slopped in the pool.

Puppets all!

Where eyes remained open in stark terror and shock, Andres closed them. Ten, fifteen bodies—and still not Juan. At the sixteenth, however, as the corpses rolled into light, Andres staggered back.

'Don Chailey!' He was certain. There could be no mistake. The fair hair. The mark of the beatings: his swollen eyes, his smashed nose. 'Don! The bastards . . . the bastards!'

74

He dragged the American to shore. He felt inside the wallet pocket of Don's brown leather jacket.

Nothing.

In turning the body over on to its face, Andres discovered his hands were covered in blood. Don's wallet was gone, his jacket pockets empty. He tried the photographer's rear trouser pocket—and struck lucky. The Black Berets were so keen to send you into the next world, Don, they didn't search you properly.

He found Don Chailey's press card. It bore his picture and proved him an accredited photographer of the *Baltimore Express & Times*. Tucked behind the card was a snapshot of his family—his wife, and two small girls.

There was also a page ripped from a reporter's notebook and folded. The paper was soaked with water. Very gently Andres opened it out. The words, written in ball-point pen, were smudged but readable: Saturday, approx. 7.30 p.m. Silver Lion murdered by agent of Security. Arrest of Miguel supporters—fraudulent. Followed assassin. Black Peugeot. Santiago—old colonial house. Pillars in front. HQ of CNI? People call it House of Laughter. The Chileans specialise in black humour!

And there was a last, heart-felt appeal, hastily scribbled: The Americans must stop giving aid and succour to bloody tyrannies such as Zuckerman's. Our own fears are our worst enemies, not the reds . . .

Andres refolded the paper. He placed it in the plastic wallet containing the press card and the snapshot. They snatched my father from a Peugeot . . . coincidence? He slipped off Don's wedding ring. At least you were spared the torturer, Don.

Juan Larreta was not among the remaining dead. Andres felt little relief. He remembered something Diego the printer had said: 'Unless we fight back, all roads in future will lead to the House of Laughter.'

Andres nodded in agreement. Or in a pool of mud.

He collected what items he could from the dead. There were twenty-eight bodies. He had the names of seventeen. News of their deaths would give no comfort to their loved ones. But Andres knew: nothing was worse than uncertainty.

Not knowing—that is the most painful thing in the world. I must do this; report the dead. For no one else on earth will.

Beto could not believe his eyes. 'They're backing off!'

The Security truck had remained parked at the side of the road throughout the puppet show of the Marionetas de los Gemelos. Along with the children of the school of San Bernardo, they had been treated to, as Beto announced it, 'a sensational star-spangled show' featuring Silvestro the Skeleton, Orlando the Ostrich and a host of other 'top-ranking artistes' ranging from a white woolly llama to a tipsy gypsy violinist.

The twins were about to commence their repertoire for the second time around when the Security truck revved up and began to reverse down the street. 'Huh!' Beto concealed his joy. 'So we're not good enough for them any more, eh?'

'Somebody's pulled their strings,' decided Isa. 'Time for our finale.'

Happy and satisfied, the audience of children dispersed, calling their thanks, imploring the Marionetas de los Gemelos to visit every day after school.

A few pesos from passers-by, and from the children, had mounted up in Isa's green panama. 'Enough to pay for the petrol.'

Beto gazed along the empty street. 'I don't think I've ever been so scared—them just waiting and waiting. I mean, if they suspected us, why didn't they pick us up?'

Isa finished putting the puppets away. 'I only hope Andres has been as lucky.'

The special evening edition of *The Mercury* provided an explanation of the Security's sudden loss of interest in the performance of the twins' marionettes. The front-page headlines trumpeted good news from the Junta:

SECURITY IN TRIUMPHANT FIVE-HOUR GUN-BATTLE WITH TERRORISTS

Sixty Self-styled Resistance Fighters Slain in Street Shoot-Out after Secret Headquarters of Red Faction Discovered.

ONLY RING-LEADERS ESCAPE—THOUGHT TO BE SEVERELY WOUNDED.

And with special emphasis, printed white against black:

CITY OF SANTIAGO PLACED ON ALERT.

'There's going to be one almighty clampdown.' Beto had stopped the van and bought a copy of *The Mercury*. They were heading home to the mill, in thick traffic.

'Just what the Junta ordered,' said Isa laying the paper aside. 'Nobody can prove if those wounded leaders exist or not. But it gives the Security the excuse to raid every house in town.'

Beto grunted. 'I guess it's time we hung the flag from our window. The rich are doing it, so why can't we if it'll protect us from the CNI?'

Isa laughed. 'First because we don't have a flag. Second, because we don't have a window.' Her good cheer faded instantly. Her thoughts were on Andres.

Beto understood. He scooped up his sister's hand in his. 'Don't you start worrying about Towny. Remember, he's a cat with nine lives . . . Or seven, maybe six. But he'll get through.'

Isa sighed. 'Beto, if you'd been wounded . . . and you were on the run—who'd be the first person *you'd* think of who'd help you?'

There was a long pause as Beto changed traffic lanes to

pull right. Ahead, the hill of Santa Lucia, usually drifting with lovers, now ringed with troops, shone white and green and pink in the dying sun. 'You mean apart from you and the mill?'

Isa's silence pressed the message home. 'Of course—Father Mariano at the seminary.'

Isa nodded, her fingernails pressing deep into her palm. 'That's why I think I gave Andres the world's worst, stupidest advice.'

'Father Mariano?'

'Who are you?'

'Andres Larreta. My friends Isabel and Beto of the Marionetas de los Gemelos told me you'd—'

'Quick, inside, my son.'

The iron-studded wooden door of the Seminary of Our Lady of Mercy opened wide enough for Andres to slip through, then closed with a bang that emphasised the uncanny silence of the street outside.

'I have to tell you—this is not a safe refuge. If you're on the run . . .'

Andres forced a calm smile. 'Purely a social call, Father.'

Mariano looked much older than his thirty years. He was ashen white. His hair receded and there was an unhealthy flush in his thin cheeks. He did not wear a priest's robe, but an open-neck shirt and jeans.

'Isa and Beto—they are not in trouble?'

Andres shrugged. 'I think everybody I know is in trouble.'

'Then you are wanted by the police?' Before Andres could answer, Mariano recognised the name. 'Larreta? Not—'

'Juan Larreta's my father.'

'What a tragedy—the accident.'

'He was taken by Security.'

78

'Then Horacio—'

'Dead. They shot him in Dad's car.' Andres must have looked exhausted for Mariano put his arm round his shoulder.

'I never met your father, but Horacio I've known since we built mud castles in the same slum. There's a hole in the ground outside San Martino where we tied for Marbles Champion of the Universe.'

Mariano pointed towards the sloping roof above the cloisters. 'Horacio used to come and do one-man shows for us. Thanks to him, we were able to get that roof repaired last month.'

He led Andres across a kitchen garden surrounded by a pillared arcade. There was a fountain in the middle whispering soft night music. 'Smell the soup already? Sister Teresa says the Almighty gives her a nudge whenever hungry guests are about to arrive.'

Andres raised his mud and blood coated hands. 'I look like a sewer rat.'

'Wash first, then eat.'

In the small, whitewashed refectory, Andres attacked the supper of chicken broth provided him by Sister Teresa. Between mouthfuls of fresh bread and delicious chunks of chicken, Andres caught a glimpse of the wry smile on Mariano's face. He paused. 'I'm sorry—were you about to say grace?'

Mariano laughed. 'Do the Larreta's say grace? I'd be surprised considering so many of Juan's songs make fun of Mother Church.'

Andres put down his spoon. He was tired and ready to take offence. He knew Mariano was referring to Juan's recent popular song which began:

When the churchmen dine
At the richman's table
The poorman's sure
To go without.

'He's never attacked the worker-priests. Only those who—'

'Please, please!' begged Mariano, full of gentleness. 'Our differences are nothing compared to what we have in common.' He shoved the spoon back into Andres' hand. 'Eat up, Comrade.'

'I'm not a Communist either.'

'Who said you were? Is there something wrong in comradeship? Do the Communists have a monopoly of brotherly love?'

Andres relented. He toasted Mariano with a last spoonful of soup. 'Comrades it is!' He finished off his meal with an apple from a bowl decorated in the manner of the Incas. He stared at its bold, angular patterns of blue and red, keenly hoping Mariano would now ask him to tell his story.

But the priest remained uncomfortably silent. Eventually he broke the growing tension by saying, 'The less we know of your business, Andres, the better. You understand?'

Andres replied by emptying his pockets on the table. Without comment, he laid out Don Chailey's press card and the photo of his wife and children. Beside them he placed the mementos he had recovered from the other bodies in the quarry—wedding rings, a crucifix, a plastic-bound book, a letter in an envelope, an unpaid fuel bill, a paperback novel, its pages soaked yet still with a smudged, ink-written name.

Priest and fugitive stared at each other, and Andres kept on staring until he forced Mariano to examine the mementos. His eyes never left the priest's face. He dared him to resist. Finally, he took out the sheet of paper from Don Chailey's notebook. He unfolded it. He placed it, face up, on the table. He pushed it across to Mariano.

He observed the look of fear in the priest's eyes. 'Read it!' And then more softly, 'Please.' He watched the priest's face. He watched for a change in its expression. He saw only a tightening of the mouth.

Andres spoke challengingly. 'You shouldn't have let me

in. I'm trouble.' He expected Mariano to explode on him—accuse him of endangering the lives of everyone in the seminary.

Mariano's voice came out dry, faint. 'The Archbishop has ordered us to co-operate with the Junta. I am to deny all assistance to those deemed enemies of the State.'

Andres was at the table before him, like a gambler frantically protecting his winnings. 'If that's the case—'

'Easy, Andres—relax!' Mariano's hand dropped firmly over Andres'. 'Leave them, my friend. Sister Teresa will hide these things where not even the Archbishop will be able to find them. Trust us, Andres!'

Desperate for rest, Andres sat down. 'Forgive me.' He tried to smile.

Father Mariano showed him to a plain cell on the first floor, and bade Andres good night.

It was in the minutes before sleep that Andres missed Helen his mother most deeply. Her words to him as a child were a ticker-tape through his brain: 'May the old grey wizard grant you sunshine dreams.' That old grey wizard must have been on strike, for Andres' mind was like the Alameda at rush-hour. It whirled and crashed with images of the past few days. Every pulse in his body seemed to be drumming, drumming in the silence.

An uneasy sleep seemed to last barely a second before being swept aside by nightmares. He found himself off the bed, on cold seminary tiles. He was soaked in sweat.

He got up, crossed to the window and sucked in gulps of cool air. He stared out over the fountain.

He knew he had to cling on to some sort of hope. Thank God for Isa and Beto, for friends. Without them, I truly would be a ghost. I can't return to school, go to college. I can't get work. One whisper of my name . . . and I'll end up in the stadium or the prison ships of Valparaiso.

It would have been in Andres' interests at this point to

return to bed, lay his head on the pillow and attempt once more to close his mind to the world. He chose instead to linger on at the window, savouring the faint scents rising from the seminary garden—and he saw what it would have been advisable not to see.

A wounded man was being carried through the cloisters to the open door of the sick room. Mariano clutched him by the shoulders. Sister Teresa and another nursing sister held him by the legs. There was a third woman, young, holding the man's hand, scarcely with the strength to walk.

The man gave a shriek of pain as the stumbling carriers rounded the corner of the garden. In the light spreading from the sick room, Andres saw that the man still grasped a machine-gun.

And on the flagstones there was a splash-splash of blood.

'Steady . . .'

'Rest a moment.'

'Almost there, Hernando.'

'He must have a doctor, Father.'

'During curfew?'

'He's lost so much blood.'

'We'll see . . . I know someone.'

They carried the wounded man into the sick room and the door was closed behind them. Andres waited. This is becoming a habit—I'm a witness again. Father Mariano soon reappeared. He was wearing a long trench coat and a trilby and looked more like a member of the Security than a man of the cloth.

Something else the Archbishop has ordered him not to do.

Andres imagined the streets outside, and the perils awaiting any person rash enough to defy the curfew. 'Course, if he *is* a member of Security . . . Andres straightened up so abruptly that he knocked his forehead—and his patch— against the iron handle of the window. If he is . . . He found himself swallowing several times a minute. He was sweating again.

'Good evening, Capitano. I've two fat pigeons for you. Plus a few trinkets that might interest you . . .' This fat pigeon endeavoured to stay calm; not get his feathers in a twist. Just the same, Andres worked out a possible route of escape. A ridge of stone ran from beneath his window to the high rear wall of the seminary. It was broad enough to back along.

He wondered, would it be better to leave now? A bit ungracious. And ungrateful. I'll only run when I have to. As he waited, he was alert and exhausted at the same time. He remained at the window and fought to keep his head from slumping on to his arms.

The chimes of the seminary clock tolled the half hour. That's two lots—or is it three? He was suddenly listening. Here's something! Andres leaned out of the window, his legs ready to spring.

A woman.

Sister Teresa had anticipated the return of Mariano. She came out of the sick room and the stream of light which followed her helped Andres to get a clear look at the newcomer. She wore a dark mackintosh and a headscarf. She carried what was probably a doctor's bag. 'God bless you for coming,' said Sister Teresa. 'He's very bad.'

'I may not be able to do much, I'm afraid, if he needs hospital care.'

'Anything you can do to patch him up, doctor—we'd be so grateful.'

Andres stood back, out of sight. Does she know the risk she's taking? The very thought of it brought damp to his forehead. Of course she knows!

He returned to bed. He was intrigued: how many reasons did she weigh in the balance before she agreed to break curfew, risk arrest and torture, to bring comfort to a wounded stranger—a wanted man?

Better not to think about it. You decide what's right, then act. He sighed. Helen would have done the same. His eyes were closing. And so would Isa. He was drifting into sleep. She'll be worrying . . . I've got to be on those mill steps first thing tomorrow . . .

If Andres had known that the whole of Santiago had been put under siege as a result of the gun-battle between the army and Resistance fighters a few hours before, he would not have slipped back into his dreams so readily. If he had known that at this moment platoons of the Black Berets were ransacking the city for those who had escaped, he would not have felt so secure among the tranquil walls of the Seminary of Our Lady of Mercy.

He did not know that the most wanted man in Chile lay one floor beneath him. What is more, in the blissful ignorance of sleep, he had no inkling that the district outside the seminary was being systematically searched, street by street, house by house.

At precisely two minutes after the seminary clock struck five, Andres Larreta was to be brought up to date with events: there was a thunderflash of sound—of the outer door battered, of shots aimed into the lock, of harsh shouts, of boots clattering tenfold over cloister tiles, of yells and the rustle of battledress.

'Lights!'

Father Mariano, sleepless, vigilant, stood by the corner of the cloisters. 'Capitano—stay your men! This is a house of God.'

'A nest of vipers more like! Search the building.'

Andres was up, struggling into his pants, hopping across the room. His shirtsleeve was inside out. It tore with the force of his panic. He reached the window, shoelaces untied. The window was wide open. He crouched. He could see the soldiers.

Now take your own advice—act, don't think! It would

84

need only one soldier to glance up, and I'm a gonner. He hitched himself on to the window-sill. He reached out with his right hand. He pushed forward with his shoulder. He held his breath. Half-way. Looking down, giddy. A single sound and their rifles would be on him.

Act—don't think! He shut his mind. He pressed his back to the seminary wall, still holding the window shutter. He let go. He watched his slowly moving feet and not the long fall down.

To his right, the high rear wall of the seminary. From this ridge of stone, a two-metre climb. But there were footholds.

Led by their officer, the soldiers had crashed into the sick room. Andres listened. There were seconds of silence before the shouting began again. 'Where is he, Father? Where in hell have you hidden him?'

'Hidden who? I don't know what you mean.'

'You trash! You red trash!' The officer blazed out his wrath. 'The traitor Hernando Salas—he was brought here.'

'We have no patients at the moment, Capitano, as you can see.'

Mariano's reply, in which he sidestepped the truth, infuriated the captain of the Black Berets. He was attacked. Andres heard Sister Teresa's scream of fear and protest. He had reached the end wall. He found a foothold where cement had fragmented from the bricks. They were beating up Mariano; and no doubt Sister Teresa too. Andres levered himself up on to his stomach. He heard the beating, the cries, the grunts. It mattered little how much noise he made. The soldiers had dragged Mariano out of the sick room. One of them held his arms back round a pillar. 'Give it him—give it him hard!'

Andres lay along the top of the wall, a black hump against the lightening horizon.

'There was a doctor—we have evidence. Now talk!'

Mariano was beaten across the chest with a rifle barrel. 'No doctor! No doctor!'

Andres slipped over the wall, holding himself with crooked fingers. A long drop—but what alternative was there? He fell as he heard Mariano's scream. He fell past the sound, away from it, into a black alley. They're killing Mariano and I'm running away! The jolt of body with ground was almost silent but caused an inner blast as Andres' left knee gave him an uppercut and sent him sprawling over grit and stone. He was upright, quivering but in one piece. Hobbling but advancing. The alley clothed him in blind darkness. Made it! The seminary wall was well behind him. Another near miss. Another closed chapter. He felt pain and a candleflame of elation.

Then: 'Halt!'

Andres slowly raised his hands above his head.

'Do not move, boy!'

Four Black Berets stared along the barrels of their rifles, each one trained on Andres Larreta's heart.

Six

In Santiago, and all over Chile, the mass arrests continue throughout the night. Helicopters whirr under bright stars, scouring the city rooftops with searchlights. Armoured cars chase shadows at breakneck speed. Tanks crush corner pavements, swinging their cannons down empty streets.

District by district, the hunt for the escaped Resistance leaders continues. In the name of this pursuit, soldiers break down doors, beat up those who protest, take many away. They plunder many secrets harboured behind closed gates: people in hiding are flushed out and taken to awaiting trucks.

And in the wake of the troops, follow the vigilantes, the Death Squads of citizens who commit atrocities under licence from the Security. They choose their own routes about the city, and their own methods of terror.

They burn. They kill. They celebrate.

'God bless the Junta!'

Isa shot up from sleep as though the roof were caving in. 'Something's happened! Something's happened to Andres.'

Beto lunged from his bedroll behind the mill door, thinking they had been attacked. 'Where—where are they?'

Isa was beside him. 'Get up, Beto. We must do something—'

'Angel, it's . . .' She was clutching him, pulling him up. 'It's a dream!'

She would not release him. 'They've got him—I know!'

Beto closed his hands round his sister's face. He closed his elbows in along her arms, holding her firmly. 'Sis, you've been having a nightmare. It's a quarter past five in the morning. And if anything *has* happened to Towny, we can't stir from here till curfew's over.'

'To hell with curfew.' She wrenched herself away. She started to get dressed. 'If it's only a nightmare—good. But I'm going to the seminary to make sure.'

'Not till after six!'

'Now!'

It was Beto's turn to dive across the room. He grappled with his sister. They overbalanced and crashed on to the floor. His weight and his determination calmed her. 'Hey . . . Andres doesn't need help from panickers.' He was amused. He stared at her, easing his grip but not shifting his position till he was sure her mood had changed. 'Do you know what? You and me are switching characters.'

He let her up. '*I'm* supposed to be the one who jumps in feet first without thinking. *You're* supposed to be Miss Cool, working things out.' He sighed. There was space between them. 'I guess you must be in love.'

'Jealous?' she said, provoked.

'A little.'

She was suddenly tender, sorry for her action and her words. 'It's just that I know—they've taken him. And I'm upset because I think we let him do too much, take too many risks.'

Beto was resolute. 'The truth is, we don't know anything. This is defeatist talk. And it's unlike you.' He paused. 'What we need is breakfast.' She beat him to the kettle and the coffee jar. 'It's my job!' Beto protested.

'Not this morning it isn't.' Isa was cheerful again. 'I want you to sit down, because I've a small confession to make. And I'd prefer you sitting down when I tell you.'

She lit the camping stove. She filled the kettle from a plastic water container. 'It's about the photographs . . . Don Chailey's pictures.'

'So?'

'Well you thought Diego had them.' She spooned coffee and sugar into two mugs.

'He does, doesn't he?' Alarm had crept into Beto's voice.

'One set of them, yes.' She watched the slow flush on Beto's face. 'And we've got the other.'

'We? But, you never . . .'

'Told you, no. In the circumstances I thought it best not to.'

'The van?' She nodded. He was up. 'You mean—those photos . . . those photos!'

'If you don't sit down, you won't get any coffee.' Isa's half-smile was bewitching but always a little sad; but her full smile was merry as a fairground. 'Now tell me, be honest, would you have kept as . . . as iron-nerved as you did when the CNI were following us, if you'd known Don Chailey's photographs were under your feet?'

Beto did sit down. He took his coffee and a hunk of buttered bread. He stared into space. 'They'd have shot us . . .'

'Probably. And now we're going to make them pay dearly for their carelessness.'

Beto gazed up at his sister, dumbly, dazedly. 'We are?'

There had been too many other prisoners for Andres to get a beating-up all to himself. Numbed with shock at his capture, he remembered little of the packed journey in a truck across the city, or of the timber hut he and hundreds of others were jammed in before the military could decide what to do with them.

They were so crushed together it was impossible to lie down, only crouch. There were as many old men as young men, too terrified to speak, except through dark, scared

89

eyes. An eerie silence. That is until an old man appealed to the guards to permit him to go to the lavatory. He was ordered to use the bucket in the centre of the hut. He protested and they dragged him out. He did not return. From that moment no one argued against using the bucket. It overflowed but still the prisoners accepted: the stench and the crush were a small price to pay for holding on to the precious jewel of life.

Accept, accept—learn to accept. Where had Andres heard that? From Juan, no doubt. So Andres accepted. He laid his head on his knees. He seemed to have nodded off for hours, though real time had moved on scarcely seconds.

Andres lifted his cheek from his knee. He turned his face. He pressed his teeth into his knee: don't drift. Don't slip away. Fix Isa's smile over the goalposts of your brain. Goalposts! That's not bad, considering. Might make a song. How about that? She kissed me once on the goalposts of my brain. It's a winner.

Yet—pain, from a blow in the back by a rifle butt; cramp in the limbs, a throbbing head. Hold—hold on. Map the future. We'll tour. The Marionetas de los Gemelos, plus one. We'll write songs, skits, plays. We'll make people laugh and clap their hands. We'll sing songs of hope. We'll resist.

He could not hold the spirit in him long. He looked about him and the shout of his defiance was a whisper, feeble and uncertain. To think, somewhere out there the sun's rising as usual.

Soon after dawn, an officer arrived with a list. He read out a dozen names. 'You will accompany me.' He spoke to the guard who thrust his way between the squatting and crouching prisoners.

'Me?' Andres blinked up at the guard.

'On your feet!'

For a breathless second Andres felt the leap of joy inside him. Were they planning to let him go? After all, he was only a sixteen year old, a boy, here among men. Yes, he would be a boy again if it suited him.

A voice behind him dismissed his joy: 'Tell us if it hurts, lad.'

The drill yard was still barbed with shadows, but the sunlight radiated above the grim barrack roofs. Another truck, fewer prisoners, two guards. No view permitted. 'Down on your stomachs!'

Andres, being by far the youngest of the prisoners, was an object of interest to the guards. 'What's he done, nicked stuff?'

'No, he's sort of special. They nabbed him at the seminary for red-necks.'

'Salas—did they find him?'

'Not a puking button of him. They must've used witch-craft.' The guard accepted a cigarette from his colleague. 'But they got the priest . . . and the Junta knows how to handle traitors who skulk behind the protection of Mother Church.'

As soon as Andres stepped from the truck he knew he had seen this place before. He had expected a prison, high walls, watchtowers; or the National Stadium itself. He had not expected a gracious house in an avenue of gracious houses, with pillared entrances and balconies.

He recognised the place from Don Chailey's photograph: welcome to the House of Laughter.

To the secret headquarters of the CNI. To the torture rooms.

Andres stood still and in cold terror. The truck had deposited its cargo of prisoners alongside the house, behind four-metre high fencing, no doubt electrified. The elegant facade of the house concealed ugly rows of prefabricated buildings to the rear, single-storey, with opaque glass windows reinforced with wire mesh.

The prisoners were lined up. 'Name!' called the officer, holding a clipboard. He repeated each name aloud, slowly, as he wrote it down. Andres' heart was ram-ramming like a loom. When his turn came he stared up into the sun: 'Benedetti.'

'Age, Benedetti?'

'Sixteen.' He swallowed. At least this was the truth.

'Full name.'

'Hugo Benedetti.'

'Identity card?'

'Lost it.'

'Lost it, *Sir*.'

'Yes, Sir. Lost it.'

The officer stared at Andres with a look which indicated he had heard this story a thousand times before. He did not answer. He signalled to the guard. 'Get them inside.'

Solitary, in the narrow cell, Andres fought to control his shivering. It's not that cold; things will be worse. It's this feeling of being cut off, of no one knowing where I am. You could tell me all about that, Juan, I reckon.

Isa will be waiting, and Beto. I've stood them up—but they'll understand. The twins are my only hope now. My candlelight in the barbed wire. Another song? Too cold to compose songs now; and too frightened.

The cell was two paces across and four deep. The concrete floor was awash, stinking. Probably overflow from sewers—or maybe these people are so inhuman that they don't even leave a bucket.

At first Andres concluded there was nowhere to sit, but as his eyes got used to the dark he noticed a board which could be let out on chains from the wall.

He sat back on the board, raising his feet from the wet ground. Nothing good's going to turn up from now on. I must accept that. I know things. Fact is, I'm a mine of information. I've got to try to persuade them that I'm useless to them.

For Andres what was to come would not be entirely unexpected. Both Juan and Braulio had suffered imprisonment and what the authorities called 'correction'.

Knowing what might happen to him was no comfort to Andres, but at least he hoped they would not take him by surprise. 'You blab,' Juan had told his son. 'You have to. You talk and you keep on talking. It's once you *stop* talking that they give you the pain. You tell them everything but what really matters.'

How, though, do you judge what really matters? And if you admit a little, surely they will suspect there is more? And when you give them more, they will demand more. Andres remembered Braulio's comment: 'For the torturer, everything is never enough.'

It was almost a relief to hear the cell door unlocked. 'Out!' Andres slipped from the bench. There was light to see the soldier drop a cigar end into the stench-water of the cell. A sharp push and Andres was in a corridor lit by naked bulbs.

He was commanded to halt at an unmarked door. They waited, each side of it, guard and prisoner, silent. The door opened. Andres was thrust in as though he had made some gesture of resistance. He felt the stirring of useless anger.

Steady, do not give them any excuses to attack you. Do not make it easy for them.

The room was long, bare, the blinds drawn, everything dark save for a powerful desk-lamp throwing a wedge of light on to an empty floor. The actors in this drama remained in shadow. Andres counted three men, possibly four, before a hood was dropped over his head.

This was a shock. He half-struggled as the hood was tightened round his neck. His arms were brought behind his back and handcuffs clipped around his wrists.

Why take all this trouble?

Suddenly, abruptly, Andres heard his own voice, as if coming from a total stranger. 'You can't do this. I'm only sixteen—the Constitution states—'

The chance to quote from the Constitution of the democratic republic of Chile was denied Andres. A fist from nowhere hurled him over, dark into dark, head and shoulder on to cold stone.

The voice of the first interrogator was calm, in monotone, difficult to locate: 'The Constitution does not extend to this place. There are no human rights here. That is why, here alone, the nation is safe from its enemies. The only privilege granted to you is to breath. It is a privilege we shall honour only so long as it suits our purpose. Do you understand?'

Should Andres say it? He could not hold back the words: 'But I *can't* breath—this hood.' Would they batter him again for insolence, for showing courage? He waited. He felt a trickle of pride, for he had broken a rule and no blow came.

'Loosen the hood.' Andres was allowed back on to his feet. 'What is your name?'

'Hugo Benedetti.'

'School?'

'No school. Moved about too much.'

'Last school.'

Pause. 'San Martino.'

'We'll check the register. Your home?'

'No home.'

'Stop stalling you little swine—answer the Doctor's questions.' This second voice was high-pitched, irritated, full of bad temper and impatience. Two voices, then. Andres named them—the Snake and the Hog.

'If you do not answer precisely,' warned the Snake, 'you will receive the treatment.'

'I'm telling you what's true.'

Hog: 'You're lying. What's your name?'

'Hugo Benedetti.'

Snake: 'We have reason to believe that is not your name.'

'My friends call me Beni—after Benedetti. Why I'm vague, well . . . my home—my parents are separated. I ran away.'

'Name of school?'

'San Martino.'

'Describe it.'

Andres knew a little of San Martino. His friend Costas had a cousin at the school. They had sometimes visited him to buy cut-price records off him. 'There are shields on the railings. One of them with the condor, and the lads are always—'

'Enough.'

Andres had the impression that the Snake was in front of him, at the desk, while the Hog prowled round him. His voice was closer, all at once at his right ear: 'What were you doing at the Seminary of Our Lady of Mercy after curfew?'

'I wasn't—'

Before Andres could continue, Snake interrupted. He too seemed to have come close. 'We shall speak of that in a moment. Tell us what you were doing before you went to the seminary.'

'I didn't go to the seminary—'

'Before!'

'I tell you I—'

Hog screamed: 'You were seen! You were captured a stone's throw from the rear walls.'

The Snake continued with his own line of questioning. 'What were you doing before . . . before you were captured?'

'Trying to find somewhere to bunk down.'

'Before curfew—the hours before curfew?'

'I was out of town.' He received a vicious blow across his head for this reply.

Hog: 'You'll have to do better than that, scum.'

'It's true. Out of town. Working, you see.'

'Working where?'

'With . . . actors. Travelling players. Scene shifting— and I sing a bit. Then when the army made its move I—'

This angered the interrogators so much that two pairs of

hands were laid on Andres. He was dragged over a chair and pinned against the wall of rough brick.

Snake, aroused: 'The army made its move—what the devil are you implying? That there was a conspiracy to overthrow the Constitution?'

'Nothing, Sir. All I know is that we weren't allowed to go on giving plays. We disbanded. I thumbed a lift back to Santiago.'

'From where?'

'San Felipe.'

'We will check. And what is the name of these players?'

It came out as though another mind was doing Andres' thinking for him: 'The Good Companions.'

'How many?'

'Five, with me—six.'

'Names.'

Andres realised, the more he lied, the deeper he dug the pit for himself. But he was set on a course now and there was no altering it.

'Names!' bellowed the Hog as Andres hesitated.

'Later,' snapped the Snake who was clearly the senior of the two interrogators. 'What were you doing at the seminary?'

'Well, the curfew—'

'What were you doing?'

'I was hungry. No idea it was a seminary—just a place I could get something to eat, maybe a bed for the night.'

'Who told you about it?'

'The lorry driver.'

'Lorry driver?'

'Who gave me a lift.'

'So you admit you went to the seminary?'

Andres had a second to decide—should he at least admit what they knew? He nodded under the hood. 'I found out it was some sort of religious place.'

'Earlier you denied being there.'

'I was afraid.'

Hog: 'That means everything you've said is a pack of lies.'

'No . . . but you are confusing me with all these questions.'

The Snake was distant again, as though he had crossed back to the desk. 'Who provided you with food at the seminary?'

Andres knew he could not go on lying, not from this point. All he could do was omit what information might be vital. What did *they* know? That was what counted now. It was to be a game of cat and mouse.

'A priest gave me food.'

'Father Mariano?'

'He did not tell me his name.'

'What time exactly did they bring in the wounded man?'

The silence was deathly. Andres could hear his heartbeat. He could hear the ticking of a clock. He could hear the Hog's thick breathing. 'The only other person I saw was one of the nuns. I went to bed and . . .' He paused.

'Go on.'

'Then the soldiers came.'

'Where did they take the wounded man?'

'I saw no wounded man.'

Hog had Andres by the jacket, lifting him, shaking him. 'The wounded man, scum, the wounded man!'

'No one—nothing!' He was slapped full in the face and his nose spilled out its blood.

The Snake's calm, relentless voice pierced the confusion of movement, and sound and pain. 'You were conveying a message from Father Mariano to the Resistance, to the remnants of Miguel Alberti's outlawed party.'

'No—no message.'

Andres was beaten from the back and from the front simultaneously. A kick behind his knees scattered him on to the ground. 'Answer!'

'No message.'

'Who did Mariano send you to?'

'What was the message? Spill the beans, boy, or we'll have your bones bouncing all over the floor.'

The Snake took a cooler route into the heart of Andres Larreta's defence. 'If you were not carrying an urgent message, why descend a five metre wall in the dead of night?'

Andres was choking on his blood. He could not staunch the bleeding from his nose because his arms were fastened behind him. He tried to tilt his head back, but the Hog had him by the hood and the hair. 'Answer the Doctor!'

'I was escaping.'

'So we agree—you were carrying a vital message.'

'No! Just escaping. There were the soldiers. Shooting. I was afraid. My room was next to the wall. I panicked.'

Snake once more approached with stealth. 'How is it that when you were captured you had no identity papers on you?'

'Lost them—in the fire.'

This answer so infuriated the Hog that he would have beaten Andres senseless if the Snake had not commanded him to leave the victim alone.

The Snake's voice soothed as it spiked: 'You must beware my colleague's temper. He has the fury of a bull when he is confronted by the red rag of the liar.'

Andres pressed on with his lie as if doing this might lend it respectability. 'The fire destroyed everything—three nights ago, all the company props, costumes . . .' His voice faltered into silence. He was down a cul-de-sac and he knew it.

'I think,' said the Snake, in unchanging monotone, 'that we have gone as far as we can with gentleness. You are unco-operative. You sing a little, yes. And you have led us a song and dance so far.' His voice was cold, like dry ice. 'You have wasted our time.'

The Snake made a signal. Other hands approached, dragging Andres up, shifting him about the room. His hands were unlocked—for that he was grateful, but they did not allow him to raise one of them to scrub the blood from around his face, now bathed in sweat.

All his limbs were grasped. They were splayed out and chained to a frame of metal, like a bed without a mattress, only upright. It is to be torture then.

This is the Pendura. I am a side of beef. They suspend me till my arm joints set alight. It is not fair: and I must not cry.

The pain Andres felt, Isa shared, in the heart, desperate with waiting. Beto had wanted to drive her to the seminary, but Isa had insisted: 'Your job's all we've got to live on.'

'It's stupid to get parted. What if *you* don't come back?'

She had ruffled her fingers through Beto's hair. 'You'll have to paint a new sign on the van—the One-Twin Marionettes.'

'Don't joke!'

Just the same, Beto had gone quietly, to help clear the debris caused by the fire-bomb that had wrecked part of the laundry premises. The owner had dared to put an election poster in his window, supporting the Silver Lion. As he admitted to Isa and Beto, 'It's the price you pay in Chile for backing the loser.'

Isa had driven through Santiago to the seminary and found the nursing sisters in mourning. Father Mariano had been taken for questioning, the seminary ransacked.

Sister Teresa, an old friend of Isa's, nursed a broken arm. Her face was so badly bruised that her left eye was not visible for the swollen eyebrow and cheek. 'I was lucky,' she said.

Of the young man who had begged shelter the night before, there was no news. 'He vanished. Escaped, we hope, but . . . Well, they say the troops had the seminary cordoned off.'

Teresa led Isa into the kitchen garden, to the fountain and goldfish pond. 'A very brave young man, your friend, Isa. He brought us some things to keep. Evidence, he said—of a massacre of prisoners.'

'Can I see them?'

They reached the fountain and Teresa smiled through her bruises. 'Over the years we've got rather good at hiding things.' She stooped and pulled out a square of stone from the wall of the pond. 'The Black Berets enjoyed themselves so much, they'll be back, so it's better these aren't found.'

She handed Isa the package of mementos, including the last possessions of Don Chailey. 'The American ambassador won't be pleased to learn that an American photographer was executed without trial by servants of the Junta. Your friend Andres saw it all happen . . . He has a nose for danger, it seems.'

Isa nodded, taking the mementos. 'It follows him around.'

'He means a lot to you?'

'He was beginning to.'

Teresa sighed. 'How often we have to talk in the past tense . . .'

Isa chose to ask, 'And Mariano—is there any news of him, Teresa?'

The nursing sister crossed herself. There was despair in her voice. 'Mariano has a serious heart condition. If the CNI torture him, we will never see him alive again.'

At the gates of the seminary, the two friends kissed each other goodbye. 'What will you do now, Isa?'

'Under the front seat of the van, I've got Don Chailey's photos.' Isa raised the mementos with reverence, as though they were communion wine. 'And I'm going to make all these things talk!'

The pain across Andres' shoulders and down his neck had

become excruciating. If only he could put his feet on the ground, touch it with his toes, ease his weight for one second.

He could smell the garlic on the Hog's breath. 'We want quick answers, you red scum, and plenty of them. We want names—get me?—names!'

Snake: 'Let us begin again. You were conveying a message. We are not particularly concerned with the nature of that message as we have a very good idea what it was. But you will now tell us to whom you were conveying that message.'

Andres' armpits were burning. The slightest movement in the rest of his body caused the pain to worsen. 'No message.' His voice was a whimper. It told him how they had reduced him in a few minutes. No points to be scored now; no victories. 'The Father just told me . . . escape . . . escape while you can.'

Yet again, the Snake altered tack: 'What is the name of the doctor who came to the seminary last night?'

'Doctor?'

Andres' whole body convulsed as he was hit in the stomach. His arms blazed with agony.

'The doctor!'

The pain was too much. 'Yes, yes . . . there was a doctor.' Andres suffered a further blow. Talking, that keeps their fists away.

'Man or . . . woman?'

'Didn't see.'

'Talk!'

'Man!'

'You lie!'

'Man!'

The interrogators backed away a step. In a rustle of voices they discussed tactics. They kept Andres hanging. He wondered, will I pass out?

Then, Snake: 'Take him down. Evidently at San Martino

they failed to teach him the elementary lessons of telling the truth—or warn him of the consequences of deceit.'

Andres was dumped on the floor.

'The wires, I think.'

'Water!' commanded Hog.

Wires and water? Andres did not need it explaining. He had heard and read enough of torture by electric shock. He knew well enough why water was being poured on the ground beneath his naked feet.

He felt a loop of wire being pressed over the big toe of his left foot. His shirt was ripped open and another wire clipped to the nipple of his right breast.

His time had come.

Seven

'Colonel Rugeros? Might I be permitted to ask an urgent question?'

At an international gathering of journalists brought together in the Ministry of Information in Santiago, an American reporter called Jack Normanton has interrupted the carefully prepared speech of a spokesman for the military Junta of Chile.

'It is about a colleague who has gone missing.'

Normanton and the other pressmen have just been informed that, following the tragic assassination of Miguel Alberti by Communist terrorists, order has been fully restored in the country. The banks are open, the wheels of industry turning as usual. Tranquillity and justice prevail once more. The curfew will continue only so long as it is absolutely necessary to destroy the Enemy Within.

What is more, the Two Hemispheres Cup competition will proceed as planned.

'My name is Normanton, of the *Philadelphia Star*, sister paper to the *Baltimore Express & Times*. My missing colleague is a photographer called Donald Chailey.'

There is nothing in Colonel Rugeros' brief which has prepared him for this question. 'I am afraid that the Ministry—'

'Chailey is missing, Sir, after flying to Santiago to cover the elections.'

The Colonel consults an adviser, a plain-clothes man wearing dark-lensed glasses. He stares down the ornate, chandeliered room at Normanton. 'We have no information on this man.'

The American persists. 'Colonel—my paper's instructions to me are to leave no stone unturned until Mr Chailey is found.'

Another reporter stands up. 'I flew into Santiago on the same plane as Don Chailey, Colonel. We booked into the same hotel. There's been no sign of him since Monday night.'

'It's our guess,' comes in Normanton, 'that he might be held in the National Stadium. So far your officials have refused point blank to make any enquiries.'

Once more Colonel Rugeros consults his adviser. He whispers. There is a firm shake of the head. He straightens up. He surveys the sea of hands, a blitz of potentially embarrassing questions. 'This press conference, gentlemen, is now at an end.'

Andres was thrown off his feet with the shock: it stabbed him along his toe, right up his leg, making him shake violently so that his knee bent automatically and his head sprang forward.

'Who else did you see in the seminary?'

'Nobody.'

Now the electric convulsions surged through his toe, up his body; and through the body from the nipple. The current seemed to have twice the power it began with. It was all through him, ripping him in all directions.

His legs caved in.

The top part of his body shot over.

He saw blue and white lightning. He was on the ground, in the wet. And he knew he could not take it. 'Mercy!'

'Mr Normanton? I have a message for you.' The American reporter of the *Philadelphia Star* had returned to the offices of the international press agency where his paper had been allocated a desk and a phone.

He was tired and angry. 'Those bastards have set a tail on me . . . Any news of Don?'

The secretary handed him a note. 'A very determined young woman phoned. A Santiaguena. She wouldn't give her name, but she said she had information about Mr Chailey.'

Jack Normanton read out the words of the message. '"Quinta Normal. Peanut seller next to the museum. Three p.m."' He smiled. 'Very cloak and dagger! What's this Quinta thing?'

'A leisure park, south-west of here. It's got a lake with boats and the museum she mentions.'

'Meet by the peanut seller, eh? Not one of the CNI's childish little tricks, do you think?'

'She was genuine. She read out the details of Mr Chailey's press card. It had a photo of his wife and children in the back . . . Oh, she told me to say you should look out for her green panama.'

Jack Normanton was thoughtful. 'Green panama? Didn't the Silver Lion wear a green panama?'

'Scum—you'll tell us the entire and absolute truth!'

'I've told it you.'

'Mariano was harbouring a terrorist—who was he?'

The shocks came again. Andres screamed again. His muscles burned, contracted. He bit his tongue. He was screaming without control, with thunder in his chest. And yet, unbelievably, his mind stayed where it was, un-molested, a little black box inside something nothing could get at. Resting like a mouse in a hole.

It surveyed the scene. It was cool, cool as early morning. It had picked up two important messages: these men did not know the name of the wounded Resistance fighter whom Mariano had helped; they might guess, but they did not *know*.

The second fact was that they did not really know who

had treated the wounded man. They suspected it was a woman doctor. Yet they had no proof. No one had confessed.

Yet.

They stopped. Andres was dizzy. The mouse in its hole was now more like a bird in a cage, somewhere out there, hanging, not part of him any longer. If they go on, if the electric continues, will my mind float off, cage and bird, through the sky of black wall?

The Snake and the Hog consulted each other once more. Then, close now, Snake asked, 'How was the man wounded?'

'I don't know . . .' Then, to head off another spasm, 'Shot, I think. I was upstairs, asleep. I didn't see.'

Hog was about to turn up the current. 'Wait,' cautioned the Snake. His voice fell almost to a whisper, but his venom was at its most potent. 'How did you know the wounded man was not Diego Rosales?'

'Not Diego Ros . . .' Andres broke off. He was falling headfirst into the trap. A fault, a crime, but his mind was so confused, the aching in his limbs so terrible.

'You knew it was not Diego Rosales, which means that you are well acquainted with Señor Rosales!'

'No—'

'Ring-leader of the Resistance.'

'No!'

A charge of electricity shuddered his body. He was a puppet, handled not with love and skill and care, but by a mad operator, his strings yanked in fury. In the chaos of his brain he seemed to feel the strings. And they were attached to his knees, to his hands, to his ears, jerking his head violently from side to side.

The Hog, with satisfaction: 'He knows. Probably knows the whole gang of them.'

Snake: 'You were running with a message to Diego Rosales, from his wounded comrade-in-hell, Hernando—

confess! You will tell us where this Diego is hiding out.'

Andres fought for control, for control of the strings. His body had no answer. The electric shocks came down the strings and the limbs answered. They leapt, they shook.

But his brain—so far they had not managed to attach a string to his brain. 'Yes I did see the man.'

'Ah, what did I tell you?' The Hog was a hyena.

'But they didn't call him Diego. I was saying . . . I don't know any Diego.'

'What did they call him?'

'Not Hernando.'

'You lie!' Down the strings came the darts of electricity. Again, in defiance of orders from his brain, Andres' mouth opened; the scream sprang forth. 'They called him . . . Horacio.' Good Horacio was dead. He alone seemed safe from the torturer.

'Horacio?' The interrogators were puzzled. Andres sensed this in the delay of their next question. Did the name suddenly strike a bell with them that they paused; did they even half believe him?

If there was any luck in this miserable world, thought Andres, he felt he deserved a grain of it.

'Horacio what?'

'I don't know . . . Just Horacio.'

A second grain of luck—the torture-room door opened. A young voice: 'We checked at San Martino, Doctor.'

Not a grain of luck after all: Andres awaited the worst. 'Very well, was the boy lying?'

'We've no information, Doctor, I'm afraid.'

'What the devil do you mean?'

'The school director was arrested yesterday, along with eight of his teachers. There is no access to records.'

'Then blow them open.'

'I'm sorry, Sir, but all the records were taken away by the assistant chief of police.'

'Zombie!'

Hog: 'What about the actors, the Good Companions—any lead on them?'

'All theatrical groups have been compulsorily suspended, Sir, by order of the Junta.'

'There'll be a register, man—no actors were permitted to practise without a licence.'

'We're working on it, Sir. But the whole entertainment business has gone to earth.'

Snake was coldly furious. 'Everywhere you look, treachery. I tell them, we shall never exercise control, win obedience, make this nation great through discipline, till we have more treatment centres, till we have access to the entire population.'

'Yes, Doctor . . .' The messenger swallowed nervously. 'The worst news, Sir, is that Mariano is dead.'

'Dead? We hardly touched him.'

'Father Mariano suffered from an acute heart condition, Sir.'

Hog, unconcerned: 'We were not to know.'

'Not to know?' The Snake's voice climbed the scale, from the cool to the trembling. 'Not to know? It was our job to know.' His voice became a screech. 'We killed him!'

'Number Two killed him, Doctor, not us,' corrected Hog.

'He died in my care.'

Andres was astounded. He could not believe what he heard. Here was the chief torturer mourning over the death of one of his victims.

The Snake was up, pacing the torture room. 'No man has ever died at my hands. I pride myself in that. They suffer a living death. They confess. I break them—but they do not die.'

Hog now seemed to have taken on the role of the smooth, unflappable interrogator. 'Did Mariano make his confession?'

The messenger scraped a boot nervously on the stone ground. 'To his Maker, Sir . . . But not to us.'

Andres' spirit was a shooting star, raking the blackness with light.

'Nothing?'

'He maintained to the end, Sir, that he gave shelter to a man named Horacio.'

Silence.

'Did he tell you this boy's name?'

'No name, Sir. Just a street urchin, he said, hiding from the guns.'

The roles of the interrogators were once more reversed. The Snake had faded, become extinguished, his interest gone. But the Hog flung off all control. He seized Andres. He roared not as the hog, not as the hyena but as the bull. He seized Andres as if suddenly he were all prisoners, as if he represented every wrong answer, every defiant spirit every act of simple courage, every refusal to betray a loved one, every resistance to tyranny. He beat him. He dragged him. And yet it was his own cries which were the loudest, his own wailing; his boundless despair.

When the Snake next spoke, the Hog ceased his beating. Even this seemed to be an act, a performance, something prearranged. A last kick hurtled Andres Larreta into unconsciousness. .

The Snake had returned to his desk. He sat behind the yellow beam of light. Only his hands were visible. His long white fingers locked together. 'Get out of here! And take that . . . that street urchin with you.'

The Junta had not so far prohibited the sale of roasted peanuts, and in the great park of the Quinta Normal the peanut sellers were doing good business under a bright sun.

Soldiers stood guard near the museum but not at the entrance to the park, as Jack Normanton paid off his taxi and looked about him.

He was not surprised at the apparent calmness of Santiago despite last night's wholesale arrests, despite the trail of terror left by the Death Squads. It had been the same in El Salvador, he remembered: in the capital city, spending as usual; in the countryside, the army butchering the peasants in hundreds.

Of course Chile was different. So officials never stopped asserting. Chile was civilised, not like El Salvador or Guatemala or Nicaragua or Bolivia. 'Contrary to what the Junta's enemies say,' declared the morning edition of *The Mercury*, 'our rulers are firm but fair. There are no political prisoners in Chile. There are no torture chambers, and reports of so-called Disappearances are lies spread by Communist infiltrators.'

The Mercury, however, warned its readers to be ever-vigilant: 'The Enemy Within remains powerful, and the loss of certain liberties is a small price to pay for the nation's self-defence.'

One of the Enemy Within was watching Jack Normanton as he strolled over to the peanut seller closest to the museum. She was also watching two soldiers at the museum entrance.

The peanut seller served from a pram-like vehicle, the upper part of which resembled a boat, and the peanuts were being roasted on the boat-deck.

Jack Normanton bought a portion of peanuts. He glanced up through the blue film of smoke and saw Isa, in her green panama, in the shade of a plantain tree.

Without hurrying, nibbling as he went, Normanton moved as far away from the view of the soldiers as possible. At the boating lake, he stopped. He sat down on an iron chair by the water.

He turned his face into the sun; he saw her coming, darkish-skinned, long-legged, slender, her features shadowed by the green panama that rested aslant long black hair. She sat beside him. She carried a plastic carrier-bag which she placed protectively between her feet.

She did not look at him. 'Are we safe?'

Normanton grinned. He took the tension out of their meeting. 'I'm not going to answer a stranger's questions unless I'm given the secret password.'

Isa smiled. 'I'm talking in whispers . . . will that do?'

'Very catchy. And very good advice at this moment. Are you wanted by the police?'

'I would be if they knew what was in this carrier-bag.'

'About Don Chailey?'

'You could have been followed.'

'I took three taxis. Lost them after the second . . . Can I buy you a coffee while we talk?'

'I think we're safer here, if you don't mind.' Isa told Jack Normanton about the mementos Andres had rescued from the dead in the quarry. She handed him Don Chailey's press card and photograph. 'Andres hid out last night at the Seminary of Our Lady of Mercy. He told them the story before . . .' She broke off.

'I know—the seminary was raided. The Information Bureau fervently deny it, but everybody knows they took the priest, Mariano.'

'It was my fault!' Isa stared fiercely at the water, twisting her knuckle in the palm of her other hand. 'I sent him there.'

Normanton spoke gently, consolingly. 'Your fault that a house of God was plundered in the middle of the night?' He paused. He sat back. 'Means a lot to you, eh, this young man?'

Isa met the reporter's eyes for the first time. Instead of replying, she fished in the carrier-bag once more and drew out a large buff envelope. 'You can print these on your front page—if you dare!'

With tremulous excitement Jack Normanton sifted through Don Chailey's photographs. He whistled in amazement. 'I can't believe it! Je-sus!'

'Can you use them, Mr Normanton?'

'Use them? They're world news. They'll be on every front page from Alaska to Australia.'

'In return, will you help me find my friend Andres, and his father Juan Larreta—please!'

'Everything I can do, I will do.'

'There's one more item.' Isa produced Don Chailey's camera. She did not immediately hand it to Normanton, a brief hesitation the reporter was quick to observe.

'Keep it for your friend Andres,' he said, returning it to the carrier-bag. 'After all, Don gave it to him. And it's well deserved.' The reporter was up, exhilarated. 'These pictures are a cause for celebration—how about some of those roasted peanuts?'

There had been no celebrations, no treats for Andres Larreta, and no treatment for his injuries. Dumped, rib broken; maybe more than one. Eyes swollen, flesh to the bone; blood in trickles from his hair, his nose. Groin afire with pain.

Half-conscious, mouthing words yet inaudible. Words of terror, of nightmare. Slung into wet. Lying, strings loose.

Tough guy?

Andres the puppet, performance ended, fallen from his one-wheel bicycle, without applause. No songs. No more songs. No arm strong enough, no fingers unlocked enough, to strum the charango. Blue lightning and white. And finally black.

Out.

Back at the mill, the twins exchanged heated words. 'But Isa, I thought you'd be pleased.'

'If things were different, of course I'd be pleased.'

'We'd only be away a couple of nights. It's work—two performances, a good audience. And we need the fee!'

'I won't leave Santiago till I know for sure what's happened to Andres.'

'We might never know.'

'Then I'll never leave!'

'That's stupid.'

'So be it—but I won't desert him.'

'Look, we owe it to the orphange in San José. We promised them a show.'

'We owe more to Andres.'

Beto stood up. He clattered the dinner plates together. 'I knew it would happen. Sooner or later.'

'Knew what would happen?'

'It doesn't matter.'

'I want to know—what would happen?'

Beto sat down on the bench, his face a mask of woe. 'If you can't guess, then I'm not telling you.'

She moved from the mattress where she had been sitting. She rested her elbows on Beto's knee, and she looked up at him full of love. 'You think Andres has come between us—that I'm more concerned about him than I am about you?'

He shrugged. 'Than us . . . The puppets. Our life. Everything we used to—' Isa rose and stifled his complaint with a pitying, caring hug. Her arms were tight around him, her lips against his cheeks.

'Idiot!'

'Maybe so . . . Yet three of us, Isa—will it work out? Don't they say three's a crowd?'

Isa's hands framed her brother's face, her thumbs hovering above his mouth as if to censor more words of doubt. 'Whoever *they* are, I'm sorry for them. It's not love if other people get pushed out. And love's not something that gets smaller if you divide it up. I'll never believe that!'

Beto was soothed, though still on his guard. Isa understood. And she accepted, she had been too swift to reject his idea, too careless of his feelings. 'Okay, you win. First we do a show at the San Miguel market tomorrow—then we treat the orphans at San José.'

Beto's mask of woe vanished. 'Really?' His natural bounce was back. 'I'll tell you this, Andres would approve. After all, he's a partner now, isn't he?'

Isa kissed her brother. 'Yes, a partner.'

Darkness, and a military truck left the gates of the House of Laughter, heading south and west towards the Maipo River. A truck carrying a human cargo of prisoners who had outlived their usefulness, some already dead, others so close to death that the difference was of no importance.

Towards the river, and along it for several kilometres, then swinging on to its shallow, white-stone banks. There, the dead and the dying were tipped like refuse; left under the cold stare of the stars. Bodies upon bodies.

Utterly motionless—save for one hand, an arm, weakly but relentlessly dragging at the pebbles. And then a leg, slow, disengaging itself, tugging, working with the arm, heaving, scraping, rolling out from under.

Free; to prove it, a foot splashing in a ribbon of oil: Hugo Benedetti, alias Andres Larreta. A cat half way through its ninth life.

He lay on his undamaged arm. There was a hoop of iron through his chest. His dislodged ribs, perhaps. He felt a coolness and in the dim shadow of his floating mind he sensed water; and the message reminded him his foot was bare, his foot still burning from the electric.

He heard the mouse in the hole in his head and it was scratching. It was saying, they've let you go. That can only mean one thing: you're not going to pull through.

He suspected a lot was broken. His arm maybe as well as a rib or two. But my spine, my legs? His good arm worked for him. It gave leverage to his back. There was pain, but not agony. Shift your legs. Try them. Go on, move. The muscles at first refused to co-operate. Am I paralysed? His head dropped back on the shingle. He was exhausted.

I've just not got the strength. His throat was opening and closing, emitting a sound half like a cough, half like someone choking on a plum stone. He rested. I mustn't sleep. Mustn't nod off. Can't actually die if I'm awake. He forced up his head again. He gazed at his companions. They were asleep and they were dead. His chin touched his chest. His eyes were almost shut.

No! I'm not ready. I've things to do. Andres Larreta lives! Half lives. He raised a knee. It worked. He raised the other knee. Bless you both!

Yet he flopped down once more, gutted of energy and strength. Rest but don't sleep. He rolled his head slowly. In the night mist he could see the twinkle of city lights. I've got to put distance between me and my compañeros. They'll not be missing me. I'll be safer alone.

One Good Samaritan is all I need. In the meantime, his good arm worked for him again. It propped him up.

In the morning, I'll thumb a lift.

He was up on his knees. They held. His back held, stiff. If I'm asked what happened to me, I'll say . . . 'It's a long story!' In agony, painfully slow, grunting, Andres set his engines going. He whipped himself with words: shift, blast you—heave! Gallop, you lazy load of horse dung. He was up, dizzy, swaying, tall as El Plomo, capped with eternal snow.

He moved. One pace. One for Juan. Stop, sway. Another pace. One for Horacio. One for Braulio. One for Don. And for Isa? Ah! He sucked in breath. He stumbled forward, across the shingle on to the grey-white stones, the sky above him swinging like a boat in a storm.

Don't look up.

Don't look down.

Straight ahead. Focus. Grit those teeth. But they hurt. I think I've lost one. Where the river bends—that's your aim. Away from the corpses.

'Done it!' This far. It's a miracle, legs. A miracle, feet. There ought to be cheers, yet there's silence; and I think I'm falling . . .

'Papa! Papa—look!'

At the top of the shore, framed in early morning light, stood a girl, about eight years old. She stared down the white shingle of the Maipo. She had hoped to see a shark—one of those her brother had told her about, which swam up from the ocean on moonless nights. Instead, she was about to save the life of Andres Larreta.

'Papa, it's a dead boy!'

'Come away, Rosa.' Her father, a farmer from the south west, was filling up the radiator of his old, open-back van, loaded with produce for market. 'It's none of our business.'

But Rosa was already skidding down the mud bank to the pebbles. She slowed as she got near the body, still as a shadow. 'Papa—Papa. I think he's alive.' She was close enough to touch Andres, sprawled on his left side, cradling in sleep his wounded right arm. She woke him with her footfalls on the pebbles.

'Are you really, really alive?'

Andres opened one eye, then the other. If he had not been in such pain he would have laughed. But to laugh—he knew—would kill him. Yet he tried to speak. This girl was his hope. His only one. 'Not really really,' he croaked. 'Just really . . .'

'What happened to you?'

Andres' mouth opened. It shut. He merely gawped at her out of listless eyes. 'Fell over.'

'Just fell over?'

'Fell over San Cristóbal . . . please!'

'Papa—Papa! He's so hurt.'

The farmer had come down, but he did not venture as close as his daughter. He was wary, afraid. He said nothing.

116

'We've got to help him, Papa.'

The man stood, a shadow in shadow, though his panama was touched by the sun edging above the giant wall of the Andes. 'You'd better come now, Rosa. We can't get involved.'

'Oh Papa—no!'

'We've the stall to put up. We must be moving.'

'But he's hurt . . . like Tonio.'

'Tonio's dead. Come now.'

'Please!' called Andres.

'I'm sorry. I'm a poor farmer.'

Yet Rosa persisted. She stayed her ground. 'Tonio had no one to help him . . . he would want us to help this boy.'

'Rosa!' The farmer was torn between compassion and fear. 'You don't understand.'

'He is like my brother. My brother's dead—so we help him.'

'Like Tonio—but not Tonio. These are bad times.'

'We help,' insisted Rosa, stubborn, underlip stuck out, eyes brown and round as buttons.

The farmer had begun to walk. His daughter followed, clutching his arm. 'Rosa . . .'

'Why not, Papa?'

'The Proclamations—I read them to you, didn't I? If this boy is wanted by the authorities and we help him, then we are traitors. We can't afford to disobey the orders of the Junta.'

'You hate the Junta, Papa. You spit on the names of the generals. The soldiers of the Junta killed Tonio.' Her hands still kept her father's arm in bondage. She hung on it. 'We do this for Tonio!'

'But the market, Rosa.'

Market? Andres stirred. He lifted his head from the pillow of stones. 'San Miguel?' The blood in his veins had seemed to have stopped flowing, no longer rivers but canals.

He was suddenly recharged. He raised himself. There was a show to see at San Miguel: the Marionetas de los Gemelos. He coughed out the words, 'At the market . . . my friends!'

The farmer stared at Andres. Indeed he did resemble his son Tonio—his thick, shiny black hair, his handsome eyes. He made his decision but not before he had scanned the riverbanks for watchers, for spies. 'Fetch the first-aid box, Rosa, and the wine. Quickly!'

Andres felt the farmer's sinewy arms reach under his back and his legs. He was up and carried, lowered gently on to the tufted grass in the shade of reeds.

'Bullet wounds? No. A beating up?'

Andres tried to smile. 'Slipped on a banana skin.' He quivered as the farmer touched his arm.

'Okay, okay . . . And your ribs?' He sighed. 'You badly need a doctor.'

Rosa returned bearing a much-dented black box which had to be prised open with a penknife. It contained bandages, lint and a large bottle of methylated spirit. She handed her father the wine.

'I think this will do you more good than bandages.' Andres choked on the first gulp yet gathered enough breath to swallow a second. 'Take it slow.'

Andres felt the wine sweep through him, driving out the shivers.

At last, he was back among friends.

Throughout his interrogation, Andres had managed to keep his true identity, his name, a secret. One day the authorities would acknowledge that a certain Hugo Benedetti was missing, believed dead. That made two of him gone; two of the Disappeared.

Now, though, Andres did not wait to be asked. 'I'm Andres, son of Juan Larreta.'

The farmer had started strapping up Andres' ribs with elastic bandage. He paused. 'Larreta? The singer?' He sat back on his haunches. He shook his head. 'A tragedy, that accident.'

'My father's alive!' retorted Andres, almost fiercely. 'But he dines out with the CNI.'

The farmer made the sign of the cross. 'God protect him, then.' He took a moment from his bandaging to clasp Andres' hand. 'And to think, we nearly didn't stop for the son of Juan Larreta. Hear that, Rosa? You can tell your Mamma . . . And maybe for once she'll admit her Francisco did a sensible thing.'

He laughed. 'More wine, Andres. And I shall have a drop myself. Fetch some cheese, Rosa, the bread and the meat— for this day we celebrate!'

Eight

Dawn, Sunday. It is a little over a week since the killing of Miguel Alberti. Though the armed forces have not yet captured all of the Silver Lion's friends and supporters, the prisons of Chile are full. They have arrested politicians, trade unionists, poets, priests, scholars, factory workers, journalists, teachers, farm labourers, lawyers, by the thousand.

There are many dead, many awaiting 'treatment' at the hands of the overworked torturer; and there are many streets yet to be searched. To the faceless servants of the Junta the order has gone out: death to all who oppose.

Leave is cancelled for the army, the police and Security until Hernando Salas, leader of the so-called Resistance, and a long list of his accomplices have been arrested. Santiago is under military occupation: there are road-blocks on all routes into the city as the morning traffic begins to roll.

Every vehicle is being stopped and inspected.

The soldiers are tired, hungry, bored; and in their harassed, feverish eyes is the threat of sudden death.

If it wasn't for the pain in my ribs, I reckon the pain in my arm would be unbearable. Andres lay under an oily blanket wedged between wooden crates of vegetables, eggs and fruit. He was being bumped, bounced, rocked and shaken, for Francisco's van had long ago cracked all its springs.

He was overwhelmed by heat and the whiff of onions.

His eyes stung. The gas was beating up his nostrils. Worst of all was the effect of the wine he had drunk on an empty stomach. While restoring a semblance of strength in him, it had flushed through Andres' brain, propelling it away from his control like a boat without oars.

If the damned army come anywhere near me, I'll breath onions and wine over them, mow them down. The Junta'll be so scared they'll take the next plane to Timbuctoo.

His head was adrift, and with it, his voice.

What are you doing?

I'm going to sing.

The Junta have banned singing.

But the voice was out there, disobedient, trilling one of Juan Larreta's forbidden songs:

> 'When Crocodile the Torturer
> Demands the name of your friend,
> When you hear your loved one was
> Burnt like toast on the Barbecue . . .'

'Hush, lad!' cried Francisco through the open window of the cab. 'The military aren't holding auditions for opera singers.'

'Sorry.' Andres shut his eyes.

Everywhere, as Francisco drove through the suburbs of Santiago towards the commune of San Miguel, tanks stood guard. Routes began to converge and traffic thickened.

'Security ahead!' called Francisco.

Andres' voice had made another dash for fame. Here—come back! But it was too late:

> 'There's a rich man up my nose
> There's a rich man down my pants
> Every place I wander
> There's a rich man in my light . . .'

This time Francisco's yell was stern: 'Shut it! Unless you really want us stuck up against a wall.'

Andres grappled with the clown that had leapt from the wine like a genie. The van was slowing. Andres heard the scrape of army boots on the roadway. He turned his head to hear more.

'Papers . . . Gratias. Destination?'

'San Miguel market, officer.'

'Stallholder's certificate?'

'All there.'

Andres felt the sweat trickle from his forehead to his ear. His arm and ribs were throbbing, the surfaces of his throat sucked dry, bonded. This is worse than being at a concert— I'm about to cough. Concentrate! On something, on anything. He clamped his eyes shut. Those blue carpets of flowers in the desert, after the rain showers. A miracle.

'Just veg on board? Let's see.'

'Fruit. A few chickens.'

Andres' mind at last obeyed. It concentrated. It moved as lightning back to the House of Laughter, to the torture room.

'Your child?'

'I'm Rosa.'

'You're overloaded, do you know that, farmer?' Traffic was piling up behind the van. The soldier hesitated. 'I ought to book you.'

Francisco shrugged. 'Things are hard. If I don't sell all I've got—'

'Papa, see! There *are* sharks.' Rosa was down from her side of the cab, pointing. 'Sharks, like Tonio said.'

Francisco and the soldier gazed along Rosa's dancing hand. 'There, there!' Below their noses, concealed only by a wisp of straw, was Andres' foot.

The soldier grinned. 'Well, I'll be damned. She's right!' On the far side of the Avenida, a long-backed lorry had halted for inspection by the commander of the patrol. It carried not only sharks but a swordfish, a small whale, a sting-ray and several dolphins. 'Sharks all right, child,' laughed the soldier. 'But stuffed sharks. Don't worry, they'll not bite your arms off at the elbow.' He called across to the driver of the lorry. 'Puttin' 'em back in the Pacific, eh?'

The driver found it hard to joke with a man armed with a machine-gun. 'They're for cold storage,' he replied, nervous.

'Where from?'

'Museum of Natural History. It's been shut down.'

'Nobbled by the bloody navy more like.' The soldier had forgotten all about Francisco's overloaded van. 'Those pansies—they think they run the whole shooting-match.' He gave Rosa a swing in the air before planting her back in her seat. He slapped the roof of the cab. 'On your way, farmer!'

For Andres, the motion of the van became like a dark opening, a cavern, the mouth of a tunnel, approaching him at speed. Is it sleep—or something worse? I must hold on, yet I am sliding. My arm is useless. My good arm seems to be trapped. Locked behind me.

Hold. You must.

I am dying.

Hold fast. But to what? He was sliding, slithering—and then all at once there was a foothold. And the foothold was Francisco singing one of Juan's songs:

'In the forests of the city
I wandered
And people touched my arm
We're lonely, we're lonely
For the truth.'

The vast market square of San Miguel was already chock-a-block with stalls. Hundreds of coloured awnings were in place and scores more were being unrolled as protection against the hammer of the sun.

'Andres, lad—can you stand up?'

'I think he's asleep, Papa.'

'We'll have to move him or there'll be sunstroke to add to his troubles.'

Andres felt a dash of water over his face. It helped. He licked at it. He turned his head away from the sun. He heard his own voice. 'Give us a hand—I'll manage.'

'These trousers, get them on. Gently now. Stand against me. Good arm over my shoulder. That's the way.'

'Got trousers.'

Francisco wasn't arguing. He lifted Andres' left leg and removed the badly-torn trouser, mud covered, blood soaked; then did the same with the other leg.

'Can't pay . . .'

'Belt's included. Now the jacket. Doesn't match the trousers, but at least there's no blood.'

'Myself, I . . .'

Andres overestimated his ability to raise even his good arm. He missed the arm of the jacket. It was the shadow again. He could not focus on the hanging sleeve and Rosa had to guide his hand into it.

'We'll leave the other, Rosa. Just put it over his shoulder.'

'I'll manage . . .'

He didn't manage. He gave weight to his legs and his legs flopped under him, weak as blankets. Francisco lowered him against the front wheel of the van.

'Is he dying, Papa?' Rosa stood in a golden frame of light. 'Don't let him die!'

Is this it, then? Can this really be . . . the feeling of limbs melting to water? Eyes open! Keep them that way. But people sometimes die with their eyes open. In the quarry they did.

Still, death's quicker with eyes shut. That's got to be a fact.

He was conscious of other faces than Francisco's and Rosa's staring down at him, of the stallholders, swarthy farmers, a plump lady in a black shawl, a youth stripped to the waist, an old man with a cane. Their images shuffled together, shimmering in and out of the light, in and out of focus.

'If he's on the run, Francisco . . .'

'Just a lad—had an accident.'

'Been beaten up, more like.'

'Kicked to pieces, poor sod.'

'You'd best keep him out of sight, friend. The place is crawling with Black Berets.'

'And Security pigs in plain clothes, waiting to cart folks off to the Villa Grimaldi.'

'He'll not be wandering far.'

'By the looks of him, his days of wandering is over.'

Enough of whispering. 'I am Juan Larreta's son—Juan Larreta!'

'Hush, Andres.'

'It's true. But . . . according to the Junta, I'm . . . I'm already dead and buried. So don't worry yourselves about me.'

No one answered. No one moved. Juan Larreta—the words had cast a spell. There were nods now, though nothing was spoken. The circle broke up. A hand reached down. It patted Andres on the head. 'Courage, lad.'

'Good luck to you then, Juan Larreta's son.'

'I once worked down the mines. Larreta gave us a free concert when the bosses locked us out.'

A bottle of wine was thrust to Andres' mouth. He tried to shake his head. I'm already drunk almost to death. Yet he took a sip so as not to offend. 'Gracias.'

'You're welcome. Keep it—keep it.'

The stallholders would not leave till they had shaken the hand of Juan Larreta's son. Then they dispersed to their stalls as the trickle of early customers became a pressing crowd.

Francisco's hands were under Andres, propping him up. 'We're going to be busy, son. You sit in the cab and rest. Okay?'

Andres obeyed. In the cab he pulled up his knees and lay crouched on the bench seat. He covered his head with his good hand to prevent the sun boring a hole through his skull. Here's the shadow. Here's the cave mouth. Here's where the printing press is buried. Only you know where it is, son of Larreta. Only you will make the printing press speak. You and Isa together. And Beto.

'Papa! Papa!' Again it was Rosa who wrested Andres from the creeping talons of the undertakers. 'Papa—there are puppets! Please, please let me go and see them . . . There's a silly skeleton. And its head keeps flying up and knocking the man under the chin. Please, Papa!'

Andres stirred. Puppets?

'Isa . . .'

He tumbled on to his bad arm. The agony cracked open his eyes. They beamed with hope, with joy. It's got to be. Isa! He pressed his head out of the cab window.

'Francisco—Francisco, por favor!'

'Rest, my young friend.'

'No, no—the puppets . . . Los Gemelos—my friends!'

'It's risky to move—dangerous.'

'It's my chance. Let Rosa take me. Please!'

'You're in no fit state—'

Andres was quivering with life. 'I could jump over El Plomo on one leg. Let me!'

Francisco pulled open the van door. He extended an arm round Andres' waist. 'El Plomo can wait till we get your feet facing in the same direction. Lean on me.'

The shadow had retreated, yet the world swam and circled. This was sea-sickness and flu rolled into one. There was more wine at his lips. He gulped at it. The ground beneath him rocked.

'Get your balance, son.' Francisco released his grip. Andres swayed, but he did not reach out for support. 'Not bad . . . Rosa, take him!'

A small, eager star of flesh slipped into his palm, grasping him with fierce strength. 'Ready, Andres.'

'Slowly, child, take him slowly—steady!'

'Of course, Papa.'

'Bless you, Francisco. And all my thanks!'

'God go with you, son of Juan Larreta!'

How am I doing this? How am I walking the tightrope between the housetops? Mustn't look down. One foot at a time. Makes sense. One foot in front of the other.

But this pain . . .

It burns. It beats. It throbs. I am cold yet I am sweating. My head's like a shower. I can't see. The light is a shadow. It is a truncheon. My shoulder is screaming. My ribs are falling down my inside. All of me is collapsing. Like Horacio's concertina.

Rosa saved him a dozen times from pitching headlong between the market stalls. She was a prop of steel. Without her, the whole mine would come down in thunder. She was in him, part of him, a substitute for his ribs. He followed her movements, her pauses, her acceleration, her turning sideways.

They had walked through a red mist of shadows into the strangest, the wildest of sounds: into a chorus of laughter. In Santiago, where hundreds had been shot, thousands arrested, where the cries of the tortured fell on deaf ears in the showers of the city stadium, in cellars below Londres Street, on the top floor of the Military Academy, in the prison ships off Valparaiso—laughter? Have people gone mad?

'There, Andres! It's a hungry ostrich now. He's pecking a lady's nose.' The laughter was that of adults as well as children. It swelled, and through it pranced the tune of the quena played by a girl, dark and tall and fresh as the morning, in a white blouse and an embroidered skirt of vertical red and black stripes.

Andres could see nothing, but he heard. You've made it. You beat them. You got back. To those you love. Yes, love.

Compañeros!

The voice of Beto rose in mock protest at the antics of Orlando the Ostrich. 'Now you give the señora her nose back this minute! Come on, come on, you villain, spit it out!'

Laughter, rocking; heads bobbing.

'Oops, it's disappeared. Where's that sniffling old nose got to? Can't do without a nose, eh, Señora? Whatever would you have to wipe your handkerchief on?'

'Rosa?' The half-blind man sensed the fading of light, the weakening of shapes. 'I think I'm . . .' Andres was reeling. She held him. 'Please—is there a van? Where the puppets . . .?' He staggered and he shook. The trembling had come upon him. In his knees, down his spine, at the junction of his throat and head.

'Yes, there's a van. You want—'

'Please.'

There was a surge of fresh laughter as Orlando attacked the señora's ear, pecking and sucking. 'Beau-oo-tiful ear! Sweeter than Yankee pears on the General's table.'

'Dump me at the van, Rosa.'

Beto's nerve at mentioning General Zuckerman, un-elected president of Chile, earned him a clatter of applause.

One risk fired another. A voice in the crowd yelled, 'It's the Yankees who pay for His Excellency's earrings too—but they make him wear them through his nose!'

A great cheer greeted these sentiments.

'We don't want their guns—and we don't want their bloody tinned pears either!'

Beto hesitated. He glanced at his sister. They were stirring up rebellion. Already there might be someone in the crowd carrying his words of insult to the Security; and yet he was amazed to see the puppet now brought from the van.

'Not Zuckero!'

'Yes—Zuckero!' Isa asserted. Proud as a peacock, the General strutted into the sunlight, medals gleaming, moustache fluffed and groomed, helmet polished and plumed.

In his right hand Zuckero wielded a toy sabre with a flag of Chile attached to the point.

Brother and sister had argued at length—and heatedly—over whether they should even bring General Zuckero to market. 'Being reckless won't help Andres,' Beto had cautioned.

'We have to fight, Beto. In whatever ways we can. Otherwise, aren't we accepting? Aren't we being collaborators?'

'I don't want to go to prison.'

Isa had smiled, stubborn. 'We'll keep the engine running.'

The crowd responded to the appearance of Zuckero with gasps of delight, and with laughter when he raised a hand to salute and knocked off his helmet flowing with llama wool dyed purple.

'Shame on you, General.' Immediately Isa replaced the helmet with a military peaked cap which fell straight over Zuckero's eyes.

'Arrest this cap at once,' screeched the General in a nerve-jangling voice, while Isa's lips hardly moved a fraction. 'Put it in irons. It is a traitor to the Republic.'

The crowd roared and cheered and clapped. Deeply anxious, Beto scanned their faces: was there a spy among them?

'So what's new, you old blood-sucker?' challenged the wag in the audience. 'How many widows and orphans have you made today?'

The General swung his sword so wildly in the air that he got the blade caught in his medals. 'Damned impertinence! One day the nation will thank me for thinning out the population. What's more, I alone have rescued Chile from a fate worse than death.'

The crowd jeered and cat-called.

'From Democracy, you mean,' called the wag.

'Exactly! From reds and poets and queers and meddling priests and human rights. From long hair, from untidiness, from litter-bugs, especially those who print nasty leaflets and stick them over my Proclamations . . .'

'Friends,' cried the wag, turning to the crowd. 'I suspected it all along, our beloved General is none other than Father Christmas himself!'

Isa laughed with the rest. She made the General nod his head in warm assent. 'If only this ungrateful nation would realise it, my friend. In future, thanks to compassionate Me, every single day will be like Christmas Day.'

'Then tell us, Mighty General, what you'll be putting in their Christmas stockings at the House of Laughter?'

The crowd was suddenly hushed, expectant, a little fearful.

'Lost for words, are you, General?' The crowd waited. A wreath of prickly silence encircled it, cutting it off from the hum of the market.

'I think that's enough, Isa,' whispered Beto. 'Time to go.'

Isa was remembering their mother and father—disappeared. She was remembering other relatives and friends—disappeared. She was remembering Andres.

This was for him. 'In their Christmas stockings, Señor? Why, we put the finest electricity!' There were those in the crowd who looked about them anxiously. This talk was exhilarating. It was bold. It was welcome. But it was also treason. Yet Isa persisted. 'And we put it through their toes as well!'

Andres had touched Rosa's shoulder. 'Now Rosa.' Her hand took his. She guided him. Skirting the crowd, towards the van, towards the open doors. He could hear the voices continue, but he could no longer take in their meaning. His head was a boulder on his neck.

'Here, Andres.' There was a space, a dark hole to burrow in—to die in? He sensed Rosa's lips against his cheek. He leaned forward, she steadying him, in among the solemn vigil of puppets, staring through and past him.

I'm back, friends . . . Need restringing.

Rosa lowered him, climbing into the rear of the van with him, resting on her knees as she edged him inwards, pushing an old rug under him, tidying him, finding a roll of blanket and covering him with it.

After making a pillow for him, Rosa kissed Andres again. 'Our Tonio was nice like you.' She scrambled out into a wall of sunlight.

'A million thanks, Rosa.'

She closed the van doors. She turned the handle.

General Zuckero had put the crowd into a fighting spirit. It was as though they had forgotten—or chose to forget—that he was a puppet. He was submitted to a hail of questions and comments, about loved ones arrested, about reports of bodies found along the Maipo, about the murder of the Silver Lion, about the executions in the stadium of Santiago.

Did the CNI kill Miguel Alberti, with the aid of the American CIA? Why have you shut down the universities, the hospitals for the poor, the free playschools—why? Where is my son? Where is my husband? Where is my father?

In numbers, the crowd discovered strength, yet several voices gave the signal of alarm. 'Watch out—police!'

'You'd better scram now, Gemelos,' urged the General's sparring partner. 'Or they'll have your insides!'

Two policemen were elbowing and palming a way through the market crush. Their revolvers were drawn. A woman protested as the police knocked over trays of brown eggs. She shook her fist. She was ignored.

Beto and Isa bundled the puppets behind the van seats, crumpled, strings tangled—but they had only seconds to survive.

The police were shouting, though not yet sure who their

target was. The crowd, having savoured the pleasure and the release of protest, did not obediently disperse. They had been impressed at Isa's courage in mocking General Zuckerman and his Junta, and aroused to indignation.

Instead of opening a path for the advancing police, the crowd knitted together. Isa's ally, who'd risked his own neck with his provocative comments, decided to start up the next entertainment: he invented a sudden attack of screaming appendicitis. His arms shot out, his legs sent him sprawling.

'Doctor, doctor! Fetch a doctor!'

'Doctor! Doctor!' went up the cry. Everyone wanted to help. The police were impeded, but not rejected. 'Help, Officer—that man's had an attack.'

'He's an epileptic!'

'Just keeled over!'

'Let us through!' commanded the police.

Yet it was the crowd which was in command. 'Over here, Officer. He's passed out.' The police were jammed in, thrust towards the groaning man. Imprisoned around him.

'Give him the kiss of life, Officer!'

Beto was at the wheel of the van. There was a cordon of people between him and the police. Ahead, there was space, magically presented to him by sympathetic storeholders. 'Here goes!' The engine coughed into life. He shoved the gearstick into first.

He glanced through the rear mirror—and saw one face, of a child waving. Her eyes were sad. She called something, faint, undiscernible.

'You, Sis, have gone crazy!' He accelerated, slowed, turned. 'But am I proud of you!' The market crowd had closed behind them. 'And they make me proud too—they saved us.'

Isa nodded, her face tense, flushed. She pressed her fingers together into a double-fist. 'That showed, Beto—people *can* fight back!'

'How Zuckero stirred them up!' Beto gave the van's dashboard a hearty slap. 'We did it—two little worms, two little mice!'

'If only Andres could have shared this with us.'

'He'd write a song about us—how we lifted our eyes up from the ground . . . San José, then?'

On the western edge of the city Beto was flagged down into a queue of traffic waiting for inspection. He was feeling cheerful. 'Well for once we've nothing to hide.'

Two soldiers of the Black Berets approached, one to each side door. 'Where're you heading, beautiful?'

Beto answered, 'San José, we're—'

'Not you, duck-face. I was talking to the lady.'

Isa did her best to smile. 'Duck-face is right. We're going to San José.'

'We could provide you with better entertainment right here in Santiago, gorgeous.'

Isa did not answer. She stared in front of her. The soldier also stared, challengingly. 'Too good for common soldiers, are you, princess?'

She turned and her eyes were mild, almost pitying. 'Nobody's too good for anybody, Officer.'

'I'm not an officer, just—'

'And I'm not a princess, so let's respect each other as ordinary human beings.'

The second Black Beret guffawed and banged his gun butt against the cab door. 'You tell that to our commander, Señorita. He treats us like a bunch of niggers off the slave ships.'

The first soldier did not smile, did not soften. 'Purpose of journey to San José?'

'A children's show—puppets.'

'No cabaret?' winked the second soldier. 'No strip-show for the over-eights?'

'Just puppets—an ostrich, a dancing skeleton . . .'

'Any passengers in the back?'

Beto shook his head, nonchalantly. 'Not at the last count, Officer.'

There was a long queue of traffic building up behind the van. The second Black Beret was for letting Beto and Isa pass on. The first soldier, however, remained sour and suspicious.

'We'll see.' He strolled to the rear of the van. 'You should take better care of your equipment, Mr Puppeteer.' He wrenched at the door handle. 'Costumes half hanging out.'

Isa's knee, sharp against her brother's, reminded him it was polite when Black Berets were trying to be helpful to leap down, stand at attention and be grateful.

A length of curtaining had spilled over the number plate. Beto shrugged, still utterly calm. 'Puppets are practically human . . . if they don't get the applause they think they deserve, they go into tantrums and kick things all over the place.'

The soldier bundled the curtaining back into the van. He was about to take a look inside when he saw Isa beside Beto. He gazed up from her slender brown legs to her high-templed face: truly an Inca princess.

The traffic was waiting.

He shut the van doors. He followed Isa to the cab. He watched her alight. He closed the cab door after her, almost bewitched. 'If you're not too good for a common soldier, Señorita, maybe you'd spare him just one smile.'

Isa obliged—and for a split second the air around her seemed to glow.

'Okay,' relented the soldier, his eyes never leaving Isa's. He slapped the cab door. 'Vamoos!'

After the exhilaration of escape—shock, at realising how close they had been to arrest; how close to a violent end to the life they had known. They drove in silence, trembling a little, and cold.

'What an idiot—what a duck-face I was to crack that

joke,' confessed Beto eventually. '"Not at the last count." They could have shot me for cheek.'

'True, Beto. But I loved you for it!'

Beto's tension exploded into a laugh. 'And then I go babbling about puppets having tantrums!'

Isa laughed with him. 'Kicking curtains all over the place!'

Beto roared. 'And he actually seemed to believe me!'

They left the city behind. The road rose and wound above the river between cultivated fields, orchards and plantations. With each kilometre from the city, the air grew fresher, the light somehow brighter, the colours sharper.

'You know where we're getting near, Isa?'

'We'll stop, I think.'

'If that's what you want.'

It was only seven days since the twins first encountered their friend Andres here on the San José road, though it seemed to be a century ago. They passed the spot, far below at the river's edge, where Juan Larreta's Chevy was lapped by the Maipo.

'For old time's sake,' Beto decided, 'we'll have our lunch where we first broke bread with Towny.' He pulled in towards the red shoulders of a tall, open-faced quarry.

Isa sighed. She got down. 'It's not real anymore. Nothing's real.'

Beto was gentle, lovingly tender. 'Go sit down, Sis. I'll bring the things.' He watched her through the frame of the open door. She walked up the slope to the quarry edge where she could see over the valley. She sat down. She stared out sadly, and then rested her head on her arm.

They had fought a good fight, Beto concluded, but nothing had been changed: Andres was gone. There would be no more like him.

'Poor Isa!'

A gust of fresh mountain air had done a cat-spring into the rear of the van. It bustled about the head of Andres

Larreta, bearing scents of the earth which acted on the wounded puppet like smelling salts.

He was not quite gone: in fact he was conscious.

From the rocks of swollen flesh which imprisoned his eyes, he spied a fraction of the world. It was light. It was blue. It was living.

He stirred. 'Anybody . . . anybody at home?'

It was a whisper, but it acted upon Beto like a hand-grenade in his ear. His jaw dropped open. His neck went stiff, then loose. He turned clumsily, as though the shock of hearing Andres' voice had reduced his mind and body to slow-motion. He wheeled, colliding with the open cab door.

He stared. Through the cab into the rear. Still wide open, his mouth emitted a soundless cry. He grasped the door. He broke through the slow-motion barrier by catapulating himself forward, around the van, tearing at the handle.

'Curtains! No wonder the curtains . . .'

He flung open the van doors. He stumbled forward, on his knees, reaching for the puppet that was almost human, for the puppet whose tantrum so nearly spoilt one of the rarest miracles in all Chile—an Appearance.

Beto grasped the wounded puppet. He discovered its pain, and changed a bear hug to the touch of a butterfly. 'Oh my God, Towny—what've they done to you?'

'Isa? Where's Isa?'

'Steady. Grab my wrist. Good. Marvellous. You're breathing!'

'Through a straw . . .'

'Lean on me.'

'Isa?'

'Don't fret. She's waiting.'

'I think I'll last.'

'You'd better!'

On his feet, but all his strength was Beto's.

'Can you walk, Andres?'

'Try me.'

There were tears in Beto's eyes. They had made it—yes, all three of them. They were together again. 'We'll patch you up, Towny. Isa knows how.' He kept shaking his head. 'This I can't believe . . .' They hobbled. The roar of the Maipo drowned their footsteps.

'This'll do, Andres.' He was sobbing, and somehow smiling. The two friends paused, a few paces behind Isa. Her back was turned. Her head on her knees. The unifying flow of the Maipo seemed to pass like a current of electricity between them all.

Isa raised her head. She stared out, listening as much with her eyes as her ears. She stood up, slowly, not yet turning.

Andres' own tears flopped over his lids, though his face bore a grin as wide as the Maipo.

Beto wanted to cry out with joy. Instead, he let Andres' be the first voice; let him announce his homecoming.

'I think I made it, Isa!'

EPILOGUE

In the stadium of Santiago a massive crowd awaits the arrival of the teams in the opening match of the Two Hemispheres Trophy competition. They have been treated to a march of military, naval and airforce bands, and a colourful display by American-style majorettes.

Of the thousands of prisoners once kept here, there is no sign; no indication that on these terraces the army murdered prisoners in hundreds, shot them, clubbed them to death; no clue that beneath the stadium, in changing rooms rendered spick and span for teams of many nations, men and women suffered torture, that new arrivals were forced along these corridors under the bombardment of rifle butts.

No sign, no evidence.

It seems that none of it actually happened, just as the atrocities committed after the assassination of President Allende in 1973 did not happen. The stories spread by the enemies of the Junta were lies, calumnies, invented to discredit honourable men.

The tiles in the showers are spotless; there is no blood in the gutters. No skulls were broken here.

Whatever they tell you, is lies.

There is a rapturous welcome for the home team, Chile, and also for the visitors, England, as they trot out from the entrance tunnel, flicking practice balls across the green turf. It is a welcome similar to that which greeted Miguel Alberti, the Silver Lion, philosopher and poet, candidate for the presidency of Chile, who would have sent the generals and the admirals and the airforce marshals back to their barracks if he had been elected; but who was felled by secret command of the Junta when he was within hours of victory.

The national anthems are played. The teams are inspected by the Vice-President of the Republic, the chief of the Chilean navy, accompanied by the British Ambassador, a close friend of the Zuckerman family.

No sign, no evidence. The memory is erased from here, among banners and klaxons, of the thousands conveyed in covered trucks to concentration camps throughout Chile, to the deserts of the Big North, to islands in the cold south, to Quiriquina, to Pisagua, to prisons from Arica to Magallanes.

No sign, no evidence; no sign on the British Ambassador's face of the distasteful task ahead of him in the next few days when he would be obliged to enquire—yet again—about Mr William Beausire, a British-born businessman, one of the Disappeared, and of two English tourists gone missing during the night Santiago was searched end to end in the hunt for Hernando Salas.

The hands of the Junta are guiltless of blood. In the Box of State, General César Zuckerman, aglitter with medals, sporting a moustache identical to that worn by a certain puppet of a similar name, is surrounded by ministers—every one of them in uniform, every one resplendent in medals and gold braid.

The General is relaxed. He leads the applause. Order in Chile has been restored: the right order; and all's right with the world. The sun glints on his medals.

Earlier today General César had granted an interview to the Archbishop of Santiago. He had assured the Archbishop that Security knew nothing of the priest, Father Mariano. Allegations that he had died at the hands of the torturer were a slander against the State.

The Archbishop was dismissed from the General's presence with a sharp rebuke: 'It is not acceptable to me, Archbishop, to be told that your priests take it upon themselves to be critics of the government. Church and State must be as one against the common enemy. My advice to them—and to you—is to preach a little less about human rights, and a little more about public duty.'

The white and scarlet ball is on the centre-spot. The captains have tossed a coin. The referee blows his whistle—a whistle very like the one used by the commandant of the prisoners, only the rules of the game were different.

'Your Excellency?' As the match gets under way, and England mount an attack that forces a corner, the Director of the State Information Services has hurried down the steps of the State Box. 'A matter of extreme urgency, Señor Presidente.'

'Later, later,' snaps the President, waving aside the leather document case which is thrust under his nose.

The Director of Information persists. 'Do not take my word for it, Your Excellency—simply look!' He opens the document case. It contains this morning's edition of the *Baltimore Express & Times*.

The front page story is written by Jack Normanton, recently expelled from Chile; and the front page picture, spanning five columns, is of Miguel Alberti at the moment of his assassination.

When the home team go one down to a scrambled England goal just before half-time, the President of Chile is not there to mourn it; nor are his ministers.

The State Box is deserted, except for the British Ambassador, clapping politely. The members of the Junta of the Republic of Chile have more pressing matters to discuss than football.

And at half-time, the crowd discovers there is something else to read than the match programme: hundreds and hundreds of leaflets are being passed from hand to hand. They too carry the tragic picture of the Silver Lion being gunned down by an agent of the CNI; they carry Don

Chailey's testimony, his eye-witness account of the killing.

Among those distributing the leaflets—printed on a pirate press dug up like treasure from a secret cave—are twins, one a girl in a green panama, accompanied by a youth with his arm in a sling.

All over Santiago, all over Chile, the leaflets are finding a welcome—from under the counter at newspaper kiosks, discreetly across cafe tables, furtively in dark recesses of churches; and tomorrow they will be passed around in factories, in the shipyards, down the copper mines.

Soon they will be as thick as salt flies over the warm springs of the High Plateau.

The match will continue. No Chilean would exchange a top-class game of football for a rebellion. And the traffic will still flow. The shops will go on being full, and the restaurants packed with pleasure-seekers.

But for those who resist, there will be a beginning. Once, Andres Larreta had loved football. Up there in the east stand are four empty seats which should have been filled by his father Juan, himself and his friends Braulio and Horacio. He had dreamt of seeing this great match.

The times, though, are no longer ripe for dreams. Andres bears the scars of torture. His face is straight. It is neither hard nor soft. It is the face of his age.

There is fighting to do . . .

It is no good waiting for others. There must be an end to whispering. And now. Andres surveys the crowd. He is watching for Isa—whom he loves. He smiles as he sees her green panama bobbing above the sea-ripple of the crowd.

Together.

And Beto. And Diego. All of us.

Yes, fighting to do.

And hearts to be won!

Chile have equalised. Andres cheers with his country-men. And he cheers for them. Out of the corner of his eye, he sees the soldiers within the perimeter fence of the stadium. They are trying to destroy the leaflets.

There are tears in Andres' eyes, for his lost father; but they are not tears only of despair.